This book belongs to:

_____

Leo Daily Horoscope 2023

Copyright © 2022 by Crystal Sky
www.Mystic-Cat.com

All rights reserved. This book or any portion thereof may not be copied or used in any manner whatsoever without the publisher's express written permission except for the use of brief quotations in a book review.

The information accessible from this book is for informational purposes only. No statement within is a promise of benefits. There is no guarantee of any results.

Images are under license from Shutterstock, Dreamstime, Canva, or Depositphotos.

Leo Daily Horoscope 2023

2023

JANUARY
M T W T F S S
                 1
2 3 4 5 6 7 8
9 10 11 12 13 14 15
16 17 18 19 20 21 22
23 24 25 26 27 28 29
30 31

FEBRUARY
M T W T F S S
      1 2 3 4 5
6 7 8 9 10 11 12
13 14 15 16 17 18 19
20 21 22 23 24 25 26
27 28

MARCH
M T W T F S S
      1 2 3 4 5
6 7 8 9 10 11 12
13 14 15 16 17 18 19
20 21 22 23 24 25 26
27 28 29 30 31

APRIL
M T W T F S S
              1 2
3 4 5 6 7 8 9
10 11 12 13 14 15 16
17 18 19 20 21 22 23
24 25 26 27 28 29 30

MAY
M T W T F S S
1 2 3 4 5 6 7
8 9 10 11 12 13 14
15 16 17 18 19 20 21
22 23 24 25 26 27 28
29 30 31

JUNE
M T W T F S S
        1 2 3 4
5 6 7 8 9 10 11
12 13 14 15 16 17 18
19 20 21 22 23 24 25
26 27 28 29 30

JULY
M T W T F S S
            1 2
3 4 5 6 7 8 9
10 11 12 13 14 15 16
17 18 19 20 21 22 23
24 25 26 27 28 29 30
31

AUGUST
M T W T F S S
 1 2 3 4 5 6
7 8 9 10 11 12 13
14 15 16 17 18 19 20
21 22 23 24 25 26 27
28 29 30 31

SEPTEMBER
M T W T F S S
          1 2 3
4 5 6 7 8 9 10
11 12 13 14 15 16 17
18 19 20 21 22 23 24
25 26 27 28 29 30

OCTOBER
M T W T F S S
               1
2 3 4 5 6 7 8
9 10 11 12 13 14 15
16 17 18 19 20 21 22
23 24 25 26 27 28 29
30 31

NOVEMBER
M T W T F S S
      1 2 3 4 5
6 7 8 9 10 11 12
13 14 15 16 17 18 19
20 21 22 23 24 25 26
27 28 29 30

DECEMBER
M T W T F S S
          1 2 3
4 5 6 7 8 9 10
11 12 13 14 15 16 17
18 19 20 21 22 23 24
25 26 27 28 29 30 31

2023 AT A GLANCE

Eclipses

Hybrid Solar – April 20th

Penumbral Lunar – May 5th

Annular Solar – October 14th

Partial Lunar - October 28th

Equinoxes and Solstices

Spring - March 20th 21:25

Summer - June 21st 14:52

Fall – September 23rd 06:50

Winter – December 22nd 03:28

Mercury Retrogrades

December 29th, 2022 Capricorn - January 18th Capricorn

April 21st Taurus – May 15th Taurus

August 23rd Virgo – September 15th Virgo

December 13th Capricorn - January 2nd, 2024 Sagittarius

2023 FULL MOONS

Wolf Moon: January 6th, 23:09

Snow Moon: February 5th, 18:30

Worm Moon March 7th, 12:40

Pink Moon: April 6th, 4:37

Flower Moon: May 5th, 17:34

Strawberry Moon: June 4th, 3:42

Buck Moon: July 3rd, 11:40

Sturgeon Moon: August 1st, 18:32

Blue Moon: August 31st, 1:36

Corn, Harvest Moon: September 29th, 9:58

Hunters Moon: October 28th, 20:23

Beaver Moon: November 27th, 9:16

Cold Moon: December 27th, 0:34

2023 INGRESSES

Mars Ingresses

Mar 25, 2023, 11:36	Mars enters Cancer
May 20, 2023, 15:24	Mars enters Leo
Jul 10, 2023, 11:34	Mars enters Virgo
Aug 27, 2023, 13:15	Mars enters Libra
Oct 12, 2023, 3:39	Mars enters Scorpio
Nov 24, 2023, 10:10	Mars enters Sagittarius

Venus Ingresses

Jan 3, 2023, 2:06	Venus enters Aquarius
Jan 27, 2023, 2:29	Venus enters Pisces
Feb 20, 2023, 7:52	Venus enters Aries
Mar 16, 2023, 22:31	Venus enters Taurus
Apr 11, 2023, 4:43	Venus enters Gemini
May 7, 2023, 14:20	Venus enters Cancer
Jun 5, 2023, 13:42	Venus enters Leo
Oct 9, 2023, 1:06	Venus enters Virgo
Nov 8, 2023, 9:27	Venus enters Libra
Dec 4, 2023, 18:48	Venus enters Scorpio
Dec 29, 2023, 20:21	Venus enters Sagittarius

Mercury Ingresses

Feb 11, 2023, 11:22	Mercury enters Aquarius
Mar 2, 2023, 22:49	Mercury enters Pisces
Mar 19, 2023, 04:22	Mercury enters Aries
Apr 3, 2023, 16:20	Mercury enters Taurus
Jun 11, 2023, 10:24	Mercury enters Gemini
Jun 27, 2023, 0:22	Mercury enters Cancer
Jul 11, 2023, 4:09	Mercury enters Leo
Jul 28, 2023, 21:29	Mercury enters Virgo
Oct 5, 2023, 0:06	Mercury enters Libra
Oct 22, 2023, 6:46	Mercury enters Scorpio
Nov 10, 2023, 6:22	Mercury enters Sagittarius
Dec 1, 2023, 14:29	Mercury enters Capricorn

Slower Moving Ingresses

Mar 7, 2023, 13:03	Saturn enters Pisces
Mar 23, 2023, 8:42	Pluto enters Aquarius
May 16, 2023, 17:01	Jupiter enters Taurus

The Moon Phases

- New Moon (Dark Moon)
- Waxing Crescent Moon
- First Quarter Moon
- Waxing Gibbous Moon
- Full Moon
- Waning Gibbous (Disseminating) Moon
- Third (Last/Reconciling) Quarter Moon
- Waning Crescent (Balsamic) Moon

● New Moon (Dark Moon)

The New Moon reveals what hides beyond the realm of everyday circumstances. It creates space to focus on contemplation and the gathering of wisdom. It is the beginning of the moon cycles. It is a time for plotting your course and planning for the future. It does let you unearth new possibilities when you tap into the wisdom of what is flying under the radar. You can embrace positivity, change, and adaptability. Harness the New Moon's power to set the stage for developing your trailblazing ideas. It is a Moon phase for hatching plans for nurturing ideas. Creativity is quickening; thoughts are flexible and innovative. Epiphanies are prevalent during this time.

● Waxing Crescent Moon

It is the Moon's first step forward on her journey towards fullness. Change is in the air, it can feel challenging to see the path ahead, yet something is tempting you forward. Excitement and inspiration are in the air. It epitomizes a willingness to be open to change and grow your world. This Moon often brings surprises, good news, seed money, and secret information. This Moon brings opportunities that are a catalyst for change. It tempts the debut of wild ideas and goals. It catapults you towards growth and often brings a breakthrough that sweeps in and demands your attention. Changes in the air inspiration weave the threads of manifestation around your awareness.

☽ First Quarter Moon

The First Quarter Moon is when exactly half of the Moon is shining. It signifies that action is ready to be taken. You face a crossroads; decisive action clears the path. You cut through indecisiveness and make your way forward. There is a sense of something growing during this phase. Your creativity nourishes the seeds you planted. As you reflect on this journey, you draw equilibrium and balance the First Quarter Moon's energy before tipping the scales in your favor. You feel a sense of accomplishment of having made progress on your journey, yet, there is still a long way to go. Pause, contemplate the path ahead and nurture your sense of perseverance and grit as things have a ways to go.

☾ Waxing Gibbous Moon

Your plans are growing; the devil is in the detail; a meticulous approach lets you achieve the highest result. You may find a boost arrives and gives a shot of can-do energy. It connects you with new information about the path ahead. The Moon is growing, as is your creativity, inspiration, and focus. It is also a time of essential adjustments, streamlining, evaluating goals, and plotting your course towards the final destination. Success is within reach; a final push will get you through. The wind is beneath your wings, a conclusion within reach, and you have the tools at your disposal to achieve your vision.

Full Moon

The Full Moon is when you often reach a successful conclusion. It does bring a bounty that adds to your harvest. Something unexpected often unfolds that transforms your experience. It catches you by surprise, a breath of fresh air; it is a magical time that lets you appreciate what your work has achieved. It is time for communication and sharing thoughts and ideas. It often brings a revelation eliminating new information. The path clears, and you release doubt, anxiety, and tension. It is a therapeutic and healing time that lets you release old energy positively and supportively.

Waning Gibbous (Disseminating) Moon

The Waning gibbous Moon is perfect for release; it allows you to cut away from areas that hold back true potential. You may feel drained as you have worked hard, journeyed long, and are now creating space to return and complete the cycle. It does see tools arrive to support and nourish your spirit. Creating space to channel your energy effectively and cutting away outworn regions creates an environment that lets your ideas and efforts bloom. It is a healing time, a time of acceptance that things move forward towards completing a cycle. This the casting off the outworn, the debris that accumulates over the lunar month is a vital cleansing that clears space and resolves complex emotions that may cling to your energy if not addressed.

◐ Third (Last/Reconciling) Quarter Moon

This Moon is about stabilizing your foundations. There is uncertainty shifting sands; as change surrounds your life, take time to be mindful of drawing balance into your world. It is the perfect time to reconnect with simple past times and hobbies. Securing and tethering your energy does build a stable foundation from which to grow your world. It is time to take stock and balance areas of your life. Consolidating your power by nurturing your inner child lets you embrace a chapter to focus on the areas that bring you joy. It is not time to advance or acquire new goals. It's a restful phase that speaks of simple pastimes that nurture your spirit.

◐ Waning Crescent (Balsamic) Moon

The Waning Crescent Moon completes the cycle; this Moon finishes the set. It lets you tie up loose ends, finish the finer details, and create space for new inspiration to flow into your world once the cycle begins again. The word balsamic speaks of healing and attending to areas that feel raw or sensitive. It is a mystical phase that reconnects you to the cycle of life. As the Moon dies away, you can move away from areas that feel best left behind. Focusing on healing, meditation, self-care, and nurturing one's spirit is essential during this Moon phase.

The Full Moon: How it can affect your star sign

The Full Moon shines a light on areas that seek adjustment or healing in your life.

The Full Moon is a time to bring awareness into your spirit of the areas that seek resolution or adjustment. Over time, the past can create emotional blockages in your life. The Full Moon forms a sacred space to process sensitive emotions and release the past's hold on your spirit.

This lunar vibration brings awareness to your spirit of how your emotions affect your daily life. When the Moon is complete, your emotional awareness magnifies, and you feel things more intensely in your everyday life.

The Full Moon brings a chance to go over inner terrain and connect with your intuition. She shines a light on areas that hold the most significant meaning in your life. This effect has a powerful impact on creativity, planning, and future life direction. Listening to your gut instincts helps you strip away from areas that only cloud judgment and muddy your awareness.

Leo: Your bravery will ensure you dig deep into every nook and cranny and release aspects that seek resolution in your life. It's never easy to engage in inner work. Still, it brings a sense of completeness into your spirit that gets you ready to engage proactively with life once more.

I use the 24-hour clock/military time.
Time set to Coordinated Universal Time Zone (UT±0)

I've noted Meteor Showers on the date they peak.

January

Sun	Mon	Tue	Wed	Thu	Fri	Sat
1	2	3	4	5	6	7
8	9	10	11	12	13	14
15	16	17	18	19	20	21
22	23	24	25	26	27	28
29	30	31				

New Moon

Wolf Moon

December/January

30 Friday

As you dig deeper into your future goals, you discover insight into the path ahead. Your creativity provides a treasure trove of inspiration and keeps the fires of potential burning. News arrives, which brings a refreshing change of pace as it casts a light on new potential around your social life. Being open to meeting new people banishes the clouds and promotes happiness in your world.

31 Saturday

You are ready to usher in a new journey; it brings a social aspect that offers unique and optimistic vibrations. It puts you in contact with people who nourish your spirit. It brings a valuable gateway towards a happy chapter that has you feeling more settled and secure. You are ready to attract abundance into your life, weaving a basket of success; you nurture a situation that inspires change.

1 Sunday ~ New Year's Day, Venus conjunct Pluto 5:24

Venus, the ruler of love, offers an abundant landscape when conjunct with Pluto. The energy of transformation surrounds your life, enabling you to advance your romantic life. It brings improvement to your personal life. Casting your net of dreams allows you to catch a bounty of potential. Lively discussions nurture your life and deepen the potential around your romantic goals.

JANUARY

2 Monday ~ Mercury sextile Neptune 6:53

This sextile attracts free-flowing and creative ideas that help you place the cherry on top of this year's plans and aspirations. A positive influence ahead that enables you to craft your vision for future growth and journey towards advancing life to the next level. You open a new chapter in your book of life and discover a vast landscape of possibility. You peel back the layers and reveal latent abilities ready for refinement as you grow and evolve.

3 Tuesday ~ Venus ingress Aquarius 2:06, Quadrantids Meteors runs Jan 1st – 5th

An emphasis on building stability in your home life brings a happy time of expansion that holds promise for your life. Your social life heats up and offers a vibrant landscape that links with opportunity and companionship. You find you can get out and make new friends, and this networking can help your life in many ways. Something special emerges in your life, and this enables you to carve out time to spend on developing creative projects that catch your eye.

4 Wednesday ~ Venus sextile Jupiter 9:07

This sextile attracts warm and abundant energy into your social life. A dash of luck and good fortune combined with enriching conversations improve social bonds in your life. It brings warm and friendly communication with kindred spirits. You attract good energy and possibilities, which helps you develop and advance your situation. It brings sharing thoughts and getting involved with illuminating conversations.

5 Thursday ~ Sun trine Uranus 16:43

This Sun trine Uranus transit brings positive change and excitement flowing into your world. Keeping your energy open helps spot the opportunity which assists you in achieving growth. You discover a fascinating prospect that lets you capitalize on a suitable environment. You soon will have more clarity and insight into the path ahead. It marks the start of an adaptive, adventurous, and exciting phase. It brings a journey that blesses your life.

January

6 Friday ~ Wolf Full Moon in Cancer 23:09

You turn a corner, which positions you to improve your life as you direct your energy into an area worth your time. It helps shake off the heavy vibes that may be clinging to your power. News is coming, which guides the path forward, and it does bring a welcome distraction that nurtures creativity. Getting involved with growing your life helps you smooth out the bumpy patches as you head towards a bright chapter. It unlocks a time of growth and rising prospects.

7 Saturday ~ Sun Conjunct Mercury 12:56

This conjunct bodes well for communication. It draws conversations that stimulate creativity and problem-solving mental energy. You are on the right path towards developing your life. It focuses on nurturing an emotional bond that hits a special note in your social life. It brings an emotionally vibrant and happy time. Positive energy reverberates around your life.

8 Sunday ~ Mercury trine Uranus 23:22

Mercury forming a trine with Uranus brings flashes of insight; expect an epiphany as brilliance surrounds your thought processes today. Keeping the fires of inspiration and motivation burning within your soul activates pathways to growth. It lets you work with your abilities and refine your talents to level up your skills and embrace enterprising options. It positions you in an environment that grows your life in beautiful ways.

January

9 Monday ~ Venus trine Mars 15:21

This week, Venus trine Mars raises your energy and brings a vibrant passion for life. You lift the lid on a curious choice that brings unique possibilities into your life. Information sparks a path of discovery. You can embrace the quickening of inspiration as it paints a social landscape. Being the recipient of this supportive energy does bring beams of joy into your world. It highlights a lively chapter that provides companionship, which is soft and enriching.

10 Tuesday

Something extraordinary makes an appearance in your life, which becomes an essential focus for developing your talents. Your skills and creativity usher in advancement. It brings an outpouring of artistic expression that feels good for your soul. It brings a sweet note into your life as getting back to doing what you love most draws well-being and happiness. Exploring where your gifts can take you offers a bonanza of potential.

11 Wednesday

An opportunity ahead allows you to showcase your talents. It brings a time that promotes new projects and assignments that connect with growing your abilities. Working with your creativity attracts a breakthrough that places you in alignment to develop your skills. You are on the cusp of change; it marks a time that expands your horizons outwardly. It sees you gliding forward as you capture the essence of inspiration and begin building your dreams.

12 Thursday ~ Mars turns direct at 20:54

With the planet Mars moving forward, your energy, passion, and drive return full force. As the landscape ahead broadens, it brings new possibilities to explore. An enterprising offer arrives that sets the scene to develop your skills in a new area. It forges a dynamic path that offers progression. A tried and true formula sees you using a planning strategy you have favored in the past. And let you dive into an exciting environment that offers a group aspect.

January

13 Friday ~ Sun sextile Neptune 14:11

Resources and support help you get busy manifesting your vision. You hit a home run and head for a winning streak when you discover a treasure trove of opportunities ahead. It draws a happy shift forward that lets you release areas that have caused blocks and lack of progress. Refining and streamlining your situation amplifies potential and enables you to turn a corner and head towards growth.

14 Saturday

News and invitations appear that brighten your mood. It shines a light on developing friendships and catching up with your broader circle of friends. You benefit greatly from a flurry of activity that surrounds your life. Nurturing foundations draws a wellspring of highly compatible options. It brings a purposeful and lively environment that sees things humming along nicely in your social life.

15 Sunday ~ Venus square Uranus 1:21, Last Quarter Moon in Libra 2:12

A Venus Uranus square creates a need to balance and harmonize interpersonal bonds while honoring your need for freedom and expression. It is a perfect time to focus on the basics and nurture your home environment. Indeed, an invitation arrives soon that offers a lively and active time with friends. It brings lighter energy into your social life and creates space to move in alignment with your vision.

January

16 Monday ~ Martin Luther King Day

Life heads towards an upswing as new possibilities draw a lighter energy flow around your life. It helps you chart a course towards an empowering chapter that lets you cut away from draining areas. Setting barriers does protect your foundations; it draws balance and equilibrium that brings a grounded and stable branch of growing your life to light. You tap into a journey that inspires your heart and leaves you feeling optimistic.

17 Tuesday

A gateway ahead opens new opportunities. It brings fresh energy, which rejuvenates your surroundings and offers a lighter path forward in your life. It helps you find your feet on firm ground as you develop new projects and endeavors that inspire your creativity. Improving life draws a significant influence that encourages growth and learning. It brings a new possibility that draws excitement as you get busy expanding the borders of your world.

18 Wednesday ~ Mercury turns direct at 13:12

Mercury is the messenger planet of communication, collaboration, and creative expression. Life becomes more manageable and flows more easily during Mercury's direct phase. It brings a happy environment that enables life to move towards an abundant chapter that nurtures your spirit. It brings an enriching environment that offers stability and stable foundations. It lights a path of enchantment that sees the creativity coursing through your world.

19 Thursday

A fortunate trend arrives that takes your vision to a new level. It gives you the green light to merge creativity with tangible results. An energizing influence encourages you to push back the boundaries and take advantage of all offered. Life becomes livelier and more social as you sync up with kindred spirits who understand your take on life. You link up with a happy chapter that opens to new opportunities.

January

20 Friday ~ Sun ingress Aquarius 8:26

The tides turn in your favor as a positive influence brings exciting prospects to the surface. It brings expansion that enables you to fill depleted emotional tanks with engaging conversations and a heightened sense of well-being. It lays the foundations for a stable and balanced journey. Working with your creative abilities has a profound effect on improving your circumstances.

21 Saturday ~ New Moon in Aquarius 20:54

Sharing and investing time in developing personal bonds sets the tone for a social environment that offers room for you to enjoy outings and fun times. It grows a journey that provides many unique experiences for your life. You dive into an enriching landscape that promotes harmony and happiness. It brings a lively time of social engagement and sharing. More communication flows into your world, bringing new dreams to light the way forward.

22 Sunday ~ Venus conjunct Saturn 22:12, Uranus turns direct 23:23
Chinese New Year (Rabbit)

The Chinese New Year heralds good luck and fortune. Rabbits are a symbol of growth and fertility. Ideas planted in fertile terrain will get a chance to blossom and grow. Plotting a strategy opens doors; it helps you progress toward goals and create tracks toward a winning chapter that improves your circumstances. Clear skies breeze into your life, bringing a unique path forward. It does heighten security and offers a productive and robust time of growth.

JANUARY

23 Monday

Your plans for this year take shape over the coming months, setting the stage for future growth in your creative life. It culminates in a turning point as it becomes the catalyst for growing your dreams. Working towards your vision takes this project to a new level. It brings a time of gaining traction and nailing your goals. Something big unfolds in your creative life; working towards your plans allows things to come together in time.

24 Tuesday

News and information ahead that helps you create good headway around developing a vital goal. You accomplish a great deal by being proactive and growing your life. Change is on the way; a potent mix of manifestation, creativity, and rising prospects crack the code to a brighter chapter. It lets you establish grounded foundations to grow a significant chapter in your life.

25 Wednesday ~ Sun sextile Jupiter 1:30

In sextile with Jupiter, the Sun attracts a restless vibe that has you yearning to expand your life outwardly. Good fortune lights a shimmering path forward that makes you eager to embark on a new journey. It sees improvement flowing into your world. It lands you in the lap of freedom and adventure with kindred spirits. This social environment reconnects you with friends and acquaintances.

26 Thursday

You step out on a journey that offers room to engage with your circle of friends. It provides new adventures and sets the tone for an ample time of sharing with valued companions who support your world. Your life is brimming with new energy, and this lets you transition to an expansive environment that reawakens creativity. It opens a time of discovery that enables you to get busy with friends.

January

27 Friday ~ Venus ingress Pisces 2:29

News and communication put the spotlight on growing your circle of friends. It promotes more excellent stability and harmony in your life as you nurture well-being and happiness. Engaging with a more active social life draws a replenishing note that re-stocks inspiration. It brings opportunities to mingle and catch up with friends and companions. New opportunities ahead sweep away stress and promote renewal.

28 Saturday ~ First Quarter Moon in Taurus 15:19

A social aspect ahead draws harmony and well-being into your life. It brings a time connected to magic and opportunity as it nurtures interpersonal bonds and supports growth and expansion. It enriches your life as it brings an influx of social opportunities to connect with friends and family. It jumpstarts a journey that speaks to your heart and brings inspiration flowing into your world.

29 Sunday

Your best qualities hit the spotlight as a social aspect animates your life. Sharing with friends brings extra support to your life. Amid a time of shifting sands, you find your feet in a unique landscape of possibility. A marvelous trend draws good luck to your door. You discover a new friendship that brings happiness among this expanding circle of exciting options. It brings a busy time that feels like the right direction for your life.

February

Sun	Mon	Tue	Wed	Thu	Fri	Sat
			1	2	3	4
5	6	7	8	9	10	11
12	13	14	15	16	17	18
19	20	21	22	23	24	25
26	27	28				

New Moon

Snow Moon

January/February

30 Monday ~ Sun trine Mars 1:45, Mercury trine Uranus 2:17
Mercury at Greatest Eastern Elongation: 25.0°W

You are on a continuous cycle of growth and change. Facing forward enables new possibilities to enter your life. You soon get busy resolving restrictions as you crack the code for future growth. You head towards expansion as you get involved with a new interest. It gives you rising creativity that promotes inspiration. You discover you can overcome the blocks that limit your situation.

31 Tuesday

Actively tapping into the potential around your creativity attracts a new assignment worth your time. You land in an environment ready to blossom as you head toward rising prospects. Adventure and news figure prominently as you head towards change. It lets you take your hopes to new levels as you reveal a journey that offers room to grow into a meaningful path forward in your life.

1 Wednesday ~ Imbolc

The wheels are in motion to attract incoming opportunities that help grow the path ahead. It creates an engaging chapter for exploring new avenues. Game-changing information arrives that hits an upward trend in your life. It brings the room to expand your skills into a unique area. Getting involved with developing your abilities lets you gain traction on achieving progress.

2 Thursday~ Groundhog Day

It has been a challenging time with many rapid changes. It can feel unsettling; pausing and reflecting help nurture balanced foundations. Some positive news is looming overhead as it brings a supportive environment shared with friends. Taking a break from everyday routines and engaging with activities that connect with friends draws lighter energy into your life. An invitation to mingle crops up soon.

February

3 Friday

Companionship with a friend plays an essential role in growing your life. It brings an exciting and engaging time of sharing thoughts and connecting with joy as you blaze a trail towards sharing companionship with someone who promotes harmony in your life. A positive influence carries you towards greener pastures as expressive discussions draw new ideas. It brings an outpouring of thoughts as you feel inspired by this person.

4 Saturday ~ Sun square Uranus 2:50

This positive square offers rising creativity that cultivates a new approach. Your perseverance rewards you with new options to tempt you towards growth. A big reveal lets you set sail on a voyage filled with promise. Smoother sailing marks a bold new beginning in your life. It brings a time of transformation that enables you to build your world and move in alignment with the person you are becoming.

5 Sunday ~ Venus square Mars 3:28, Snow Full Moon in Leo 18:30

This square can cause challenges as a difference of opinion fosters tension and conflict. Being flexible, understanding, and adaptive will help harmonize bonds and limit the disruption caused by Venus facing Mars at a harsh angle. Being willing to compromise will improve the foundations and limit the disruption in your life. Flexibility and adaptability improve the foundations of your social life.

February

6 Monday ~ Mercury sextile Neptune 18:27

Rational thinking and dreams align in this sextile. You see rising creativity and analytical thinking promoting epiphanies that count. This cosmic alignment helps your dreams become a reality as structured backing behind your vision offers tangible results. Life holds glittering possibilities that encourage expansion. New options advance life towards a progressive and prosperous journey that nurtures your creative abilities.

7 Tuesday

You may discover your priorities shift as you seek to change the fundamental way you approach your situation. Greener pastures beckon, which draws information that inspires rising prospects in your working life. It helps you touch down on a promising journey of evolving your situation. It does bring understanding into how you have grown through overcoming challenges.

8 Wednesday ~ Venus sextile Uranus 5:28

Spontaneity, fun, and fresh adventures rule your social life with this engaging sextile. You head towards a more vibrant and active social life. A changing scene overhead leaves you feeling excited. It brings a social aspect that offers opportunities to mingle. Expanding your circle lets you embrace a more connected and supportive landscape. It leads to a busy and active time of social engagement.

9 Thursday

Life heads to an upswing and promotes expansion in your life. It helps you go in big and think outside of the box as you develop an area that offers to become a successful path forward in your life. It takes a journey of growing the security and building foundations that build your skills as you head towards a learning time. The work behind the scenes draws advancement to your career prospects.

February

10 Friday ~ Mercury conjunct Pluto 17:16

Today's conjunct between Mercury and Pluto offers intense curiosity to delve a little deeper into life's mysteries. Doing some soul-searching provide clarity into the path ahead. A healing influence washes away outworn areas, nourishing your spirit, and opening life to a new start. A sentimental theme carries thoughts back to the past, enabling you to shut the door on an area that feels complete. Taking time to build stable foundations in your life draws a pleasing result.

11 Saturday ~ Mercury ingress Aquarius 11:22

News arrives that cracks the code to a happy chapter in your social life. It brings an opportunity to mingle as lightness and momentum carry you forward to brighter prospects. New options arrive that bring ideas and inspiration flowing into your world. It gets an active and dynamic time ahead. Impending news brings a forward-facing environment as you launch towards rising prospects.

12 Sunday

Today rules emotional awareness, and trusting your instincts helps you make the right choices as you move beyond your comfort zone and deepen a bond. It grows into a journey that offers many new experiences and paves the way for an enriching chapter ahead. It draws an engaging time that offers support and sharing. A situation you nurture takes on a life of its own and soon blossoms.

February

13 Monday ~ Last Quarter Moon in Scorpio 16:01

Improvement ahead cracks the code to building stable foundations in your life. It brings a winning chapter that draws many blessings into your world. An influence emerging helps you develop some dreams you've had on the backburner. Getting involved in progressing your vision forward illustrates a sunny aspect that brings inspiration into your life. News arrives that brings a boost and leaves you feeling excited about the potential around your life.

14 Tuesday ~ Valentine's Day

Your love life moves from strength to strength. It lets you move towards a happy chapter that brings stability, growth, and companionship. Lightness and momentum return to your romantic life as you step out on a journey that offers room to grow into an inspiring path forward. It brings a time of new adventures and setting goals. It sets the tone for an abundant landscape to emerge in your personal life.

15 Wednesday ~ Venus conjunct Neptune 12:25

Venus joins forces with Neptune, and your love life takes on a dreamy quality as you engage in fanciful thoughts and contemplation. The desire moves into unlimited imagination as you think about the future, intending to nurture romance in your life. Creativity soars under a positive influence that cultivates a unique landscape. It brings a productive and energetic time where significant change leads life forward.

16 Thursday ~ Saturn conjunct Sun 16:48

Saturn connects with the Sun to blaze a trail towards developing your goals. Getting serious about limiting distractions and cultivating discipline, concentration, and order will help you nail progress in your working life. Gaining traction on improving the security in your world will bring a valuable sense of achievement and accomplishment to your door. An influx of social opportunities enriches your life.

FEBRUARY

17 Friday

Life takes on a rosy hue when new information crosses your path. It ushers in a time that rekindles your vitality. There is movement ahead in your social life that sparks magic and potential. It brings something to be developed as thoughtful discussions open the trail towards building a unique endeavor. Friends and companions play a role in developing the journey ahead. You land in an environment that is ripe for advancement.

18 Saturday ~ Mercury sextile Jupiter 2:13, Sun ingress Pisces 22:30

The Mercury Jupiter aspect creates harmony between both planets. It sparks rising curiosity, questioning, and fresh ideas. Making yourself a priority is a gateway to growing your dreams. It brings a busy time that focuses on improving the security in your life. Evaluating the path ahead and moving away from areas that failed to reach fruition is vital in achieving gold. Creativity and inspiration burn brightly, advancing energy to new endeavors.

19 Sunday ~ Venus sextile Pluto 17:04

Today's Venus and Pluto alignment offers depth and insight into your thought processes. It helps you dig a little deeper and discover what drives your passion. Thinking about the areas that hold the most significant meaning in your life can be helpful on many levels. It weeds out the areas that no longer are a good fit for your life by letting you see the most meaningful aspects of your world. Moving in alignment with the person you are becoming nurtures inspiration and passion.

February

20 Monday ~ Presidents' Day. New Moon in Pisces 7:08, Venus ingress Aries 7:52

News arrives that brings new information to light. The conditions for advancement ripen and promote rising prospects in your life. It helps you create the solutions that lead to a breakthrough. Being adaptable and prioritizing the areas that offer gold facilitates progress and heads you towards a successful result. With a New Moon in Pisces, you can make plans that align with your emotional self.

21 Tuesday ~ Shrove Tuesday (Mardi Gras), Mercury square Uranus 22:22

Original thinking, creative brainstorming, and insightful epiphanies are the order of the day as Mercury squares off against Uranus today. Things are ready to shift forward as a new opportunity crops up that lets you channel your energy productively and efficiently. It offers new beginnings that stir creative inclinations, promoting innovative projects. Tapping into your ability to manifest goals creates rising inspiration that provides a flurry of possibility.

22 Wednesday ~ Ash Wednesday, Lent Begins, Mercury trine Mars 20:14

A Mercury trine Mars aspect attracts a restless vibe. This cosmic alignment leaves you feeling spontaneous and ready for new adventures today. Fantastic news ahead brings a refreshing option. Pursuing your dreams advances life forward in an exciting fashion. It places you in a favorable alignment to create growth as you head toward higher prospects. Stimulating new leads bolsters confidence and harnesses the energy of optimism to achieve stellar results.

23 Thursday

A busy and productive time ahead places the spotlight on developing your talents and growing your skills. It brings a fruitful direction to channel your energy as you advance to a new level of learning. The path ahead glitters with potential as you unpack a time of rising prospects that give you the green light to extend your reach. As you evolve your abilities, you blend ideas with others and develop plans that carry you forward to greener pastures.

February

24 Friday

Sharing with your friends attracts happiness and leads to a self-expressive chapter that boosts your confidence. An invitation arrives that opens a path of sharing thoughts and ideas with kindred spirits. Lightness and momentum return to your life as you step out on a journey that offers a social engagement and companionship.

25 Saturday

Opening your life up to new people and possibilities takes you on a journey that nurtures happiness and abundance. Lighter energy flows into your life, helping you build stable foundations that secure a pleasing result for your life. News arrives that has you feeling optimistic as it brings an emphasis on building your social life. It ushers in a busy time for networking and mingling with friends. A focus on your social life becomes a prominent aspect soon.

26 Sunday

Life does lighten by degrees, and a positive influence ahead helps you turn a corner. The more you push back the barriers, the more you can connect with inspiration. A new unique area calls your name and propounds you forward towards developing your talents. It gives you the green light to chase your dreams and head towards rising prospects in your life.

March

Sun	Mon	Tue	Wed	Thu	Fri	Sat
			1	2	3	4
5	6	7	8	9	10	11
12	13	14	15	16	17	18
19	20	21	22	23	24	25
26	27	28	29	30	31	

New Moon

Worm Moon

February/March

27 Monday ~ First Quarter Moon in Gemini 8:06

Focusing on the building blocks of your life brings a calming influence that smooths out the rough edges. Setting boundaries and protecting your energy is essential in achieving a balanced and harmonious environment. New opportunities ahead help release outworn energy and nurture a more grounded path. It lets you move towards a new chapter that offers increasing possibilities.

28 Tuesday

A helpful avenue opens that brings a busy time. It helps you develop your talents and nurture your skills. Gathering your resources, and planning for future growth, lets you create the stepping stones that take you toward success. A new opportunity gives you the green light to link with development and progress. It offers a cutting-edge initiative that refines your skills and amplifies your abilities.

1 Wednesday

You soon enter a more abundant landscape when new possibilities arise, inspiring change. A dream comes into focus, giving you the green light to connect with inspiration and creativity. It draws new pathways that advance your vision forward. Sunnier skies bring a lighter element into your world. This expansion cycle leads to a breakthrough that brings social engagement and happiness.

2 Thursday ~ Venus conjunct Jupiter 17:35, Mercury conjunct Saturn 14:34, Mercury ingress Pisces 22:49

Today's Venus conjunct Jupiter aspect is a positive sign for your social life. Expect an upward trend as rising prospects draw communication and invitations to mingle. As an insightful cast of characters enters your social life, you reveal collaboration and joint venture opportunities. A more active and productive pace offers a turning point that leads to growth.

March

3 Friday

News arrives that lifts your spirits. It adds a dash of spice and the element of excitement into your life. It sees you circulating more often with friends. This engaging time nurtures well-being and promotes more harmony and happiness in your life. Mingling ahead expands horizons and facilitates companionship, a wonderfully therapeutic influence. As you enjoy lighter overtones that foster engaging conversations with friends, the tides turn in your favor.

4 Saturday

Fortune is ready to shine upon your life. It brings opportunities and options that help you move towards an energizing chapter of social engagement. You can remove the doubt and stress as you build a bridge towards a happier chapter in your life. Opportunities to mingle bring improvement to your social life. It helps you expand your horizons as networking with friends introduces you to new companions worth your time.

5 Sunday

Good news ahead spotlights a trail worth investigating. It helps you set sail on a voyage that promotes happiness and joy. Extra opportunities draw closer that encourage positive outcomes. You forge a friendship that nurtures harmony in your social life. It brings a bond with someone who has an allure for life. It brings an engaging social environment that promotes expansion in your world.

March

6 Monday ~ Purim (Begins at sundown), Sun sextile Uranus 13:41

This sextile heightens creativity and self-expression. You discover a new approach that boosts productivity and offers efficiency in your daily life. Change and discovery add a spontaneous element today. Anything could crop up to provide you with a sign of newfound inspiration. A surge of unique options brings an optimistic vibe into your world. New goals and an inspiring vision help you implement functional changes that offer rising prospects.

7 Tuesday ~ Worm Full Moon in Virgo 12:40 Purim (Ends at sunset), Saturn ingress Pisces 13:03

The planet Saturn moving into Pisces is a significant shift. This changing of the Saturnian guards highlights the need for spiritual healing. It emphasizes finding meaning in your daily life and growing a solid spiritual basis to help you ride out any turbulence in your life. Evolving and expanding on this journey enables you to weather the storms and head towards sunny skies.

8 Wednesday

Taking time to pull back and contemplate your future life direction draws an exciting chapter of growing your world. It links you up with a pathway that offers room to develop your talents and nurture your abilities. Refining your gifts lets you explore a journey that feels right for your soul. It enables you to invest your time wisely in an area that is a soothing balm for your restless spirit.

9 Thursday

Improvement ahead brings a beneficial influence. New information in the pipeline draws a busy and productive time which helps you gain traction on developing your goals. Rising prospects are imminent; thinking carefully about your future dreams stirs the essence of manifestation. It helps your talents flourish as your creativity guides you towards developing a venture that offers advancement.

MARCH

10 Friday

It is a time of new beginnings that offers a fresh start in your life. Creative powers are rising as your situation transforms towards new options that amplify potential in your world. A forward-facing opportunity helps you burst forth towards developing an exciting venture. It banishes the clouds and brings the sun shining overhead. Being open to new journeys will promote wonder, curiosity, and excitement.

11 Saturday ~ Venus sextile Mars 15:04, Mercury sextile Uranus 21:04

Venus has your back today and draws social engagement. Change orients you towards new options. Growth occurs in both your career and social life. Networking draws a pleasing result as you discover new companions worth your time. Your Life moves from strength to strength as you nurture your social life. As you dissolve the barriers, you take advantage of opportunities to mingle and invitations to share with your broader circle of friends.

12 Sunday

A social chapter ahead breathes fresh air into your surroundings. It supports a journey that involves your circle of friends. Being open to developing personal bonds in your life draws new possibilities that promote expansion. You receive information about a situation that catches your interest. It does see something important coming into your life that enriches your world.

March

13 Monday

Plotting your goals keeps you one step forward from the rest. It lets you build a life in a productive, efficient, and expansive fashion. It brings refreshing options that nurture your abilities and grow your talents. Life picks up steam, bringing the room to explore side avenues of potential. A journey of adventure and discovery tempts you towards new goals and challenges. It brings something valuable on offer that sparks advancement in your life.

14 Tuesday

Good news arrives soon in a flurry of excitement. It lets you achieve real and lasting change as it brings a focus on growth and expansion. It brings options to go beyond your everyday routine and explore new heights of possibility. An exciting chapter blooms with a refreshing lightness. It places a strong emphasis on your social life and spending time with people who support your growth.

15 Wednesday ~ Last Q Moon in Sagittarius 2:08, Sun conjunct Neptune 23:39

You may feel sensitivities rising today as the Sun links up with Neptune in the sign of Pisces today. Intuition is sparking, and you can trust your gut instincts to guide you correctly when you reveal curious information that triggers your emotions. It helps establish strong bonds as you network and enjoy mingling with friends. Progressing life draws happiness and harmony into your world as you get involved with nurturing your life.

16 Thursday ~ Mercury conjunct Neptune 17:13, Sun square Mars 18:09, Venus square Pluto 19:58, Venus ingress Taurus 22:31

Today, you may feel chaotic and under pressure as a great deal of cosmic energy disrupts stability in your life. Expect intensity as the Sun square Mars alignment may leave you tense and hot under the collar. Creative expression and taking time to make yourself a priority will be beneficial in releasing frustrations and any heavy energy clinging to your spirit.

MARCH

**17 Friday ~ St Patrick's Day. Mercury square Mars 4:48,
Sun conjunct Mercury 10:45, Venus sextile Saturn 20:25**

Today, Venus sextile Saturn promotes cooperation and offers the chance to join a joint project. Striking while the iron is hot helps put plans into action. You receive an important message that provides a missing puzzle piece. It gives a refreshing landscape that lets you move forward with growth plans. Newfound power propels you forward towards developing your vision.

18 Saturday

You connect with someone friendly and sociable who brings the news flowing into your life. It draws a sweet note into your world as this person offers up lively discussions and has a happy outlook on life. Life gathers momentum, and being open to sharing with another offers support and stability. It brings a vibrant social environment that is a boost to your spirit. It delivers bright and cheerful news that leaves you smiling.

19 Sunday ~ Mercury ingress Aries 4:22

You soon enter a social chapter that expands life outwardly. It lays the groundwork for a more connected future as lively discussions bring an enriching chapter to light. It heightens emotional well-being and supports your world with thoughtful conversations that bring new possibilities to light. It helps you plan for future growth by bringing news and information your way.

..y ~ Sun sextile Pluto 20:12, Sun ingress Aries 21:20,
..ara/Spring Equinox 21:25

New options arrive soon, which brings a lift into your life. It lets you transition to a happy phase where you see improvement and progress. A clear path opens to guide you towards rising prospects. An area you nurture and develop a picks up speed, bringing your dreams into focus. Being open to new possibilities becomes the gateway from which you grow your world. Forward momentum carries you towards an extended time of advancing goals.

21 Tuesday ~ New Moon in Pisces 17:22

It has been an unsettling time, but focusing on the building blocks helps draw in new energy that sweetens your life as you reach rising prospects. Creating a stable platform from which to nurture your goals becomes a priority. It helps you turn a corner and enjoy smooth sailing ahead. It brings companionship, and this promotes a valuable support system.

22 Wednesday ~ Ramadan Begins

Being in touch with your thoughts and having a clear vision of the path ahead will help you step out on a journey of rising possibilities. It symbolizes new beginnings as unlimited options help transform your life. Developing your skills and increasing your knowledge enables you to chart a course towards greener pastures in your career.

23 Thursday ~ Pluto ingress Aquarius 8:42

Add a spark of ambition into the mix of today's ingress to achieve a golden outcome. New goals take shape under this positive influence, bringing a pleasing result. It helps you strike out on a new path that expands your horizons. It brings something new as you head into the unknown and embrace living in the moment. Creative enterprises emerge to grow your talents and evolve your abilities.

MARCH

24 Friday

Today reveals a fortunate trend. Understanding this potential helps you make things work in your favor. It takes you to a chapter of developing your dreams and exploring a social aspect with kindred spirits. It lets you step into a lighter time and embrace a social environment filled with engaging conversations. You begin to see the path ahead more clearly and find your feet in a new landscape.

25 Saturday ~ Mars ingress Cancer 11:36

Taking stock helps you re-evaluate your life and trim the less viable areas ready to be released. Exploring pathways enables you to unearth new options that promote social expansion. You soon discover a climate ripe with possibility. Keeping open to expanding your horizons connects you with a broader environment that supports social engagement. It brings an opportunity to share thoughts and ideas with kindred spirits.

26 Sunday

Today's mindfulness offers an intuitive understanding of your future dreams and desires. It helps reveal secret or hidden information that places you in alignment to grow your life. It jumpstarts a unique area that sparks growth as it draws a highly productive cycle. It enables you to extend your reach into a new venture worth your time. It brings expansion, personal growth, and rising prospects into your world.

MARCH

27 Monday

Your talents and services are in demand, bringing substantial growth to your career trajectory. Life delivers a message that you are ready to explore further opportunities worthy of your time. Assignments and projects crop up to grow your abilities. It brings a time of contemplation as you have several avenues worth exploring. It brings a beautiful time that lights creativity and inspiration.

28 Tuesday ~ Mercury conjunct Jupiter 6:49

This astrological conjunct is perfect for brainstorming as ideas are big and expressive under this planetary influence. You direct your attention to a journey that advances your talents and refines your abilities. Working on your plan for the future gets everything ready to launch. Making tweaks and refinements is instrumental in drawing the best results possible. Your flexibility and creativity are valuable tools that help you chart a course toward achieving your dreams.

29 Wednesday ~ First Quarter Moon in Cancer 2:32

A lucky break arrives and paves the way forward towards nurturing goals. It helps establish potent creative energy, and this spark helps you engage your skills to bring your life into harmony. Drawing magic power from your spirit enables you to create a journey that is your chosen path. Now is the time to begin making plans, to start a new project that inspires your mind.

30 Thursday ~ Mars trine Saturn 19:03, Venus conjunct Uranus 22:25

Mars forms a trine with Saturn today to give your working life wings. Hard work, dedication, and perseverance improve the day-to-day foundations of your life. Venus teams up with Uranus to add a dash of spontaneity to your social/personal life. As you set out on a new adventure, staying true to yourself will keep you aligned with the person you are becoming.

April

Sun	Mon	Tue	Wed	Thu	Fri	Sat
						1
2	3	4	5	6	7	8
9	10	11	12	13	14	15
16	17	18	19	20	21	22
23	24	25	26	27	28	29
30						

New Moon

Pink Moon

March/April

31 Friday

Spending time away from challenging or problematic areas will recharge your life force and help you create positive change. Focusing on improving your circumstances brings a magical time that offers rising prospects. It leads to a new journey forward in your life that promotes change. It brings a bigger goal to light; the impact of this venture carries you over the coming months.

1 Saturday ~ All Fools/April Fool's Day

A piece of the puzzle falls into place when you reveal new information about the path ahead. It brings stable foundations that give you a feel for future options. A fresh outlook draws a pleasing outcome. It connects you with inspiration, and a fresh flow of ideas soon flows into your world, offering a revitalizing aspect. Opening the book to a new chapter heightens creativity; it connects you with kindred spirits keen to nurture the possibilities.

2 Sunday ~ Palm Sunday.

Nurturing your life cracks the code to drawing balance and well-being into your world. It sparks inspiration that enables you to discuss ideas with friends and colleagues. Sharing with your social network draws benefits as new options soon appear tinged with gold. It ticks the right boxes to initiate an endeavor that brings movement and discovery.

APRIL

3 Monday ~ Mercury ingress Taurus 16:20

You are on track to improve your life by exploring different leads. A new area of growth ahead inspires growth and highlights an abundant landscape of possibilities for your career path. It would be a fresh start that offers room to develop your skills and deepen your talents. It provides space for progression and heightened security in your working life.

4 Tuesday

Your excellent judgment helps you reach for goals that inspire you creatively. It positions you to achieve growth as you head towards developing your dreams. You embark on a journey that offers fantastic rewards as it brings a pleasing result into your life. It helps give you a glimpse of the abundance ready to blossom.

5 Wednesday ~ Passover (begins at sunset), Mercury sextile Saturn 16:18

With Mercury in sextile with Saturn, communication skills are rising. Enhanced clarity and mental insight help you understand more significant concepts, thought processes, and ideas with ease today. This cosmic enhancement enables you to step beyond traditional or repetitive learning and take your studies/working life to the next level. It helps you rise to the challenge and pole vault successfully over the hump day.

6 Thursday ~ Lent Ends. Pink Full Moon in Libra 4:37

Looking into the complexities that surround the situation broadens your perception. It helps you achieve a sense of closure that nurtures well-being. It shuts the door on a problematic area that feels done with for now. Indeed, new potential soon flows into your life, drawing an empowering chapter. It brings the room to nurture a bond that inspires growth and harmony. It paves the way forward toward a fresh start.

APRIL

7 Friday ~ Good Friday, Venus sextile Neptune 17: 59

Today's planetary alignment offers a mindful, spiritual aspect that is in keeping with the spirit of Easter. Venus sends loving beams into your home and family life, harmonizing bonds and drawing the essence of rejuvenation and renewal. Connecting with a lively environment adds momentum to your goals. It provides plenty of motivation to expand and grow in a new direction.

8 Saturday ~ Mercury sextile Mars 6:23

A sextile between Mercury and Mars sharpens cognitive abilities today. Mental clarity is on the rise, giving you valuable insight into the path ahead. It lights up avenues of success and prosperity as you turn the corner and head towards lucrative options worth your time. A renewed sense of purpose drives your vision forward with momentum and clarity. Building your dreams offers advancement as you extend your reach into new areas.

9 Sunday ~Easter Sunday

Life brings opportunities for collaboration that draw harmony and abundance into your world. It lights a path of social engagement, joint projects, and enterprising endeavors that use your talents and make the most of your abilities. Helping out another brings a stabilizing environment that draws balance to your foundations. It brings a calming influence that smoothes out the rough edges of your life. It lights a positive path toward starting a new venture.

APRIL

10 Monday

You have an eye for detail and can ferret new information. Having a flexible perspective and emotional awareness helps you stay on top of the game. Opportunities to mingle ahead encourage constructive dialogues that touch on many diverse topics. It brings a new vantage point to your social life; it draws group activities that bring balance and harmony into your world.

11 Tuesday ~ Venus ingress Gemini 4:43, Venus trine Pluto 10:14, Sun Conjunct Jupiter 22:07, Mercury at Greatest Elong 19.5E

You can hold on tight and embrace the changes ahead as you unearth an enticing possibility that encourages expansion. It draws happiness and connects you with a social chapter that brings a winning environment into view. It triggers a time of contemplating the path ahead with a curious mindset. Expanding your life nourishes well-being and helps you thrive.

12 Wednesday

It is a time that brings new growth pathways into your career trajectory. Something curious is unfolding in the background of your life; it will get everything you need to feel secure as you grow your world. It brings a chance to progress your skills and develop your abilities in a new venture. You take on a new assignment that showcases your talents.

13 Thursday ~ Passover (ends at sunset), Last Quarter Moon in Capricorn 9:11

An emphasis on improving your social life draws a favorable chapter. Friends and family connect, and an option to use technology connects you with someone who has lately been out of the loop. A pioneering attitude pushes boundaries and draws higher opportunities to deepen a bond. It brings conversations that are tailor-made for renewing a situation. It sparks a friendly time of catching up and supporting one another.

APRIL

14 Friday ~ Orthodox Good Friday, Venus square Saturn 16:38

A Venus square Saturn encourages taking a personal inventory of meaningful areas in your life. Adjusting course as necessary will give private bonds the best chance of success. Shining a more intensive light on interpersonal situations in your social life helps you see the truth and cut away from outworn areas. Set firm boundaries if a drama llama is in your circle of friends. Being clear about things helps you cut away from toxic influences.

15 Saturday

Expanding your circle of friends lets, you create headway in achieving a pleasing result for your personal life. It pushes back the boundaries that have limited progress as it connects you to a broader social environment. It brings the warmth of friendship and the anticipation of fun into your world. It draws freedom, abundance, and joy. You soon turn a corner and reach a new chapter of possibilities.

16 Sunday ~ Orthodox Easter

News ahead signals that a changing, dynamic environment is ready to bloom in your social life. It turns your attention to a friendship that is a strong focus ahead. It brings opportunities to mingle and connect with someone who seeks to become closer. Giving this person advice draws a happy aspect to light that nurtures the bond of friendship. It brings positive communication and a chance to enjoy life relaxed.

April

17 Monday

A breakthrough ahead rains unique potential in your life. It creates space to focus on developing your skills. You release the past as you shake off the heavy vibrations dialed in your creativity. You discover you can truly thrive in a unique and dynamic landscape. New options become a catalyst for growth. An original and innovative journey forward rules the way of advancement in your working life as you take in a new area of learning.

18 Tuesday

As one door closes, you undergo a transition time that takes you towards a new chapter. Taking a step back and thinking about the direction ahead lets you choose your journey with forethought and clarity. The changes ahead help you plot a course towards developing your skills. It ushers in a time of growth and learning that advances your abilities, and it cracks the code to a dynamic chapter ahead.

19 Wednesday

An enterprising offer ahead lands at your feet and tempts you forward. It brings a cycle of prosperity that broadens the scope of potential in your life. It brings a fruitful time working with your abilities and nurturing your talents as you expand your horizons into new areas. It offers fundamental changes that advance your capabilities; a new role on offer sees past struggles fade away.

20 Thursday ~ Ramadan Ends, New Moon in Taurus 4:12, Hybrid Solar Eclipse, Sun ingress Taurus 8:09, Sun square Pluto 16:26

The Sun square Pluto aspect draws rejuvenation. Pluto charts a course of transformation while the Sun attracts rising prospects. This planetary combo elevates creativity. Setting intentions and thinking about future goals marks a fruitful chapter to light. It brings a busy time of building stable foundations and nurturing a progressive growth phase.

April

21 Friday ~ Mercury turns Retrograde in Taurus at 8:34

Mercury plays havoc with interpersonal bonds and can send communication haywire during its retrograde phase. Buckle up; it will be a bumpy ride as your social life goes on a Mercury-driven rollercoaster. As you navigate forward, focusing on being adaptable, compassionate, and flexible will give you a solid basis to stabilize personal bonds during this chaotic chapter.

22 Saturday ~ Earth Day, Lyrids Meteor Shower from April 16th -25th

New possibilities arrive soon that is a salve for your restless spirit. It brings a chance to mingle with kindred spirits, and a social vibe tempts you into your broader community. Discussions and decisions ahead place a focus on nurturing your social circle. It brings a happy time of mingling with friends and exploring social opportunities. It draws togetherness and a practical sense of connection.

23 Sunday

Your life has grown in many ways, and you can use the lessons learned along the way to improve your everyday experience. Incorporating the past lessons wipes the slate clean and prepares you to enter a new chapter of potential. Synchronicity guides the path ahead and harmonizes your energy as you expand your life into a new area. A serendipitous route opens, and this area connects you with a personal vision that holds meaning in your life.

April

24 Monday ~ Mercury sextile Mars 3:22

Quick reflexes enable you to spot the diamond in the rough. The Mercury sextile with Mars offers new leads. A proactive approach reshuffles the deck as you head towards a landscape imbued with possibility. It brings a chance to refine and upskill your talents. Rising prospects draw advancement, encouraging you to keep evolving and growing your abilities as new horizons tempt you forward.

25 Tuesday ~ Sun sextile Saturn 10:47

Today's sextile brings opportunities that light a path forward. It illuminates fantastic potential that enables you to improve your circumstances. Expansion ahead offers the chance to develop an area that captures your interest. It has you working on larger goals that progress your talents. It helps you break fresh ground that opens the floodgates to new possibilities. Optimism and inspiration are guiding force that sees potential surge in your world.

26 Wednesday

Taking time to make yourself a priority is essential to achieving a top result in the workplace. Little routines balance your life, and new opportunities ahead attract progress as you head towards growth. Rising prospects help you gain traction in a more stable working environment. It does bring advancement as you build upon your skills.

27 Thursday ~ First Quarter Moon in Leo 21:20

Unexpected news brings a lucky aspect that draws an enterprising chapter. It helps you find your way out of the briar patch and plant seeds that offer room to blossom into a large project. You get established in an area that needs your gifts. Using your talents and abilities to advance your potential lets you enjoy a sense of accomplishment. It draws security and creates a stable platform to initiate new projects.

April

28 Friday

You soon lift the lid on an enterprising chapter that helps you press forward towards developing an area that offers rising prospects. Working with your creativity fuels your spirit and enables you to create a bridge towards a brighter future. A refreshing change of pace arrives, connecting with your social life. It brings lively conversations and the opportunity for social engagement to become a prominent aspect.

29 Saturday ~ Mars sextile Uranus 8:04

This sextile brings unique ideas that help you think outside the box to obtain innovative solutions. Uranus places the focus on rebellion, liberation, and freedom. It adds a dash of spontaneity into your life today. Being proactive enables you to create tangible progress at a good clip. Increasing opportunities offer a compelling call to action. An emphasis on improving your circumstances launches your star higher. You turn the corner and enjoy a winning chapter.

30 Sunday

Broadening your perception draws grounded foundations as you open your life to new people and experiences. Opportunities ahead enrich your world, seeing you making progress as you move forward toward new options. It brings a project that offers room to grow your world. There is a lot of emphasis on improving your home life, which expands outwardly into the pathways that take you towards growth.

May

Sun	Mon	Tue	Wed	Thu	Fri	Sat
	1	2	3	4	5	6
7	8	9	10	11	12	13
14	15	16	17	18	19	20
21	22	23	24	25	26	27
28	29	30	31			

AQUARIUS VIRGO TAURUS SCORPIO STARS MARS SUN ARIES CAPRICORN WEDDING WEALTH FORTUNE CALENDAR GEMINI LOVE ASTROLOGY MOON MONTH HOROSCOPE LEO SAGITTARIUS HAPPINESS BIRTHDAY ASTRONOMY CANCER LIBRA NEPTUNE DATE ZODIAC PISCES SKY EARTH SIGN TODAY DAILY WEEKLY CONSTELLATION MONTHLY

New Moon

Flower Moon

May

1 Monday ~ Beltane/May Day, Pluto turns retrograde in Aquarius 18:39, Sun conjunct Mercury 23:27

Pluto is the modern ruler of Scorpio; it symbolizes how we experience power, renewal, rebirth, and mysterious or subconscious forces. This retrograde phase lasts until October. It allows you to dive deep and explore inner realms and darker aspects of your personality ordinarily hidden from view. Understanding your psyche on a deeper level provides access to the forces driving your personality. It lets you comprehend the why and wherefore behind desires.

2 Tuesday

Notable changes ahead highlight a journey that nurtures your life. It brings a healing influence that removes the outworn areas. It lets you touch down on an approach that promotes growth as you head towards rising prospects. Your confidence, drive, and creativity rise to meet the challenges of growing your life outwardly. Keeping your eyes open for fresh possibilities lets you move forward with a sense of purpose.

3 Wednesday

Life heads towards an upswing soon. It brings social opportunities bubbling along, and you enjoy a more active and vibrant engagement time. Meeting up with friends and sharing communication brings a perfect time to team up and blend ideas with others. It plants the seeds of ideas that blossom over the coming months. It brings new horizons that beckon forward, seeing your talents shine.

4 Thursday ~ Venus square Neptune 17:40

A Venus square Neptune aspect offers a dreamy quality. It provides the perfect vibe for engaging in the big sky dreaming about your perfect romantic escapade. While fairytales in the sky offer relaxation and escapism, it's important to remember that this dreaminess could lead to delusion if you overly focus on something currently out of reach. Understanding the escapism and creative elements at play enables you to dream big and still feel grounded in reality.

MAY

5 Friday ~ Venus sextile Jupiter 4:02, Flower Full Moon in Scorpio 17:34 Penumbral Lunar Eclipse

Venus and Jupiter's sextile create beneficial and harmonious vibrations for your romantic life. Good luck and rising prospects bring warmth and social engagement. It promotes networking with kindred spirits, and this cultivates well-being and happiness. Discussions and decisions ahead focus on growing your life as you connect with friends and explore incoming social opportunities.

6 Saturday ~ Eta Aquarids Meteor Shower April 19th - May 28th

Your priorities are currently shifting. It does bring change as you transform towards a busy time that helps you resolve sensitive areas. Adopting an abundant mindset broadens the playing field as it brings an approach that offers positivity. You mark a significant turning point as a social environment draws kinship and companionship into your life. It offers an upgrade that feels lighter, and this nurtures your life.

7 Sunday ~ Venus ingress Cancer 14:20

You may be feeling at a crossroads where you have a sink or swim feeling. You have the strength within your spirit to shed outworn areas and improve your circumstances. Seeing the challenges ahead as stepping stones to a brighter future enables you to make the most of growing your life in a new unique direction. You cross the threshold and transition towards a more promising chapter that marks the beginning of something big in your life.

May

8 Monday

Removing the outworn layers creates space for a new chapter of potential to emerge. The news arrives, which inspires and delights. It leads to a bold chapter where you embark on expanding your horizons. Being discerning about the path ahead helps you navigate a journey towards improving your circumstances. The winds of change blow into your life, bringing new possibilities to tempt you forward.

9 Tuesday ~ Sun conjunct Uranus 19:55

Something currently percolating in the background of your life arrives with a splash of color. It brings a boost, as it lets you combine your talents with a growth journey. Being innovative, adaptive, and proactive draws a pleasing result. It connects you to magic and possibility. You head to a time of transition that sees your potential jump to the next level. It sees you working with your abilities and refining your talents as you advance your situation forward.

10 Wednesday

You enter a dynamic time of developing goals. It brings heightened opportunities that help you hit the ground running. It rules a time of crafting your vision and creating the steps necessary to achieve your goals. A productive and active environment blends beautifully with your vision for future growth. Moving along draws balance into your foundations that create the correct stability for your life.

11 Thursday

A new option ahead leaves you feeling energized and excited about the potential. It lets you get involved in a group environment, which adds fuel to your inspiration. It sees creativity skyrocket as it draws a trailblazing time of brainstorming sessions with kindred spirits. You open an avenue that tempts you towards expansion. Listening to your intuition sharpens your instincts and lets you make a judgment call based on your gut reaction.

May

12 Friday ~ Mercury sextile Saturn 8:32, Last Quarter Moon in Aquarius 14:28

Mercury sextile Saturn gives your Friday a boost which helps you tidy up loose ends before the weekend. Mental acuity rises, bringing a focused mind and increased powers of observation lets you see what needs addressing. Today's other cognitive improvements include excellent concentration, memory, and organization skills. With everything running smoothly in your working life, you can enjoy the weekend ahead knowing you have taken care of business.

13 Saturday ~ Mercury sextile Venus 2:41, Venus trine Saturn 6:56

Mercury sextile Venus offers a social and friendly influence making this a great day to connect with your tribe. Sunnier skies loom overhead as you expand your life and grow your world. You soon team up with a friend who brings companionship and shares thoughtful ideas. Building stable foundations usher in a peaceful and tranquil environment. It underscores an atmosphere of rising potential.

14 Sunday ~ Mother's Day (US)

You turn a corner soon and head towards brighter prospects. The future looks rosy as a unique and exciting landscape nurtures new possibilities in your life. You discover a venture that captures the essence of inspiration, enabling you to forge ahead towards developing new projects. An opportunity for collaboration attracts growth and a sense of kinship in your life. It connects with an upbeat time that is lively and engaging.

May

15 Monday ~ Mercury turns direct in Taurus 3:16, Mars trine Neptune 13:44

With Mercury turning direct today, the focus is on your social life. Mars forms a trine with Neptune, enhancing potential as confidence rises and you feel ready for social engagement. It offers the perfect solution for the dodgems as you get busy being self-expressive, communicative, and creative. Nurturing your life brings expansion into view. It provides a fruitful time to increase your circle of friends. As you create headway, you connect with a happy time ahead.

16 Tuesday ~ Jupiter ingress Taurus 17:01

It is a time that carries you forward. Building new foundations let your journey evolve as you embark on developing a new approach in your life. You discover a more connected social network to explore, which brings the room to grow your life in a meaningful area. It helps you surround yourself with supportive people who offer thoughtful discussions in a lively atmosphere. It brings a time of networking that allows fresh winds of possibility to blow into your world.

17 Wednesday

You turn a corner and enter a winning chapter that elevates the potential possible in your world. Change is surrounding your life. Information arrives that orients you to explore a new journey forward. Synchronicity appears in the sign of symbols and signs that point the way in the right direction. Investigating leads brings a cycle of steady growth to your door. It gets you in sync with developing your goals as it enables you to chart a course towards success.

18 Thursday ~ Jupiter square Pluto 1:09, Sun sextile Neptune 8:59

Today's Jupiter square Pluto brings extra drive and increased energy to complete projects and finish your to-do list. Neptune also boosts your goals as a sextile with the Sun helps you find the resources and support needed to manifest your vision. You can bring your dreams to reality as the planets have your back today, attracting rising prospects into your life.

May

19 Friday ~ Mercury sextile Saturn 6:50 New Moon in Taurus 15:54

Today, Mercury, Saturn sextile boosts your communication skills and confidence. Add in a dash of New Moon inspiration and aspiration. You have the perfect mix for engaging in brainstorming with valued companions. Sharing ideas and adding creative ingredients into the pot of manifestation helps you develop a winning trajectory from which to grow your world next month.

20 Saturday ~ Mars ingress Leo 15:24

Mars lands in Leo, and this raises confidence. It's time to go big and be proud and bold. Your life opens to a broad landscape that gives you a leg upward to a more prosperous environment. It brings a time of refining and reshaping goals. It aligns you with growing your world in a new direction. Exploring pathways helps unearth a journey that marks a bold chapter of rising prospects. It brings an expansive shift that lightens life with an expressive element.

21 Sunday ~ Mars opposed Pluto 3:11, Sun ingress Gemini 7:04, Sun trine Pluto 13:58

Mars connects with a competitive edge today that could see your authority tested. The Sun trine Pluto aspect also adds fuel to the fire as it increases your desire to gain power and feed your ambitious streak. You seek opportunities to elevate your standing among peers and co-workers today. Climbing the ladder towards success becomes a dominant factor.

MAY

22 Monday ~ Victoria Day (Canada), Sun sextile Mars 5:56

The Sun sextile Mars transit brings vital energy and renewed zest for life. A refreshing aspect ahead grows the potential possible in your life as it offers solid and secure foundations. It helps you overcome barriers and move forward toward greener pastures. Personal growth and self-development lift the restraints and unlock the blocks that prevent progress. It directs your attention to a wellspring of abundance that offers happiness.

23 Tuesday ~ Mars square Jupiter 5:13

Today's Mars square Jupiter offers a positive influence that increases stamina and boosts your energy. Enthusiasm for the task at hand rises, boosting productivity and enabling you to deal with the day's demands efficiently and capably. Streamlining your environment lets you make effective adjustments that raise the potential. Pushing back the barriers and expanding life outwardly brings a defining moment that cracks the code to a brighter chapter.

24 Wednesday

Dynamic and vibrant opportunities arrive to tempt you towards expansion. It helps you initiate a path that lets you take a leap of faith towards growing your abilities. Exploring new possibilities draws sweeping changes into your life. You are reaching for something more that offers room to expand your skills. It lets you forge ahead towards an area that shows promise. It sees you moving out of your usual routine and enjoying a change of scenery which reboots your energy.

25 Thursday ~ Shavuot (Begins at sunset)

New options crack the code to a wide-open road of unique potential. It brings a social environment that dials down stress and leaves you feeling inspired. You improve circumstances as life opens up and tempts you into your broader community. It opens the gate to a brighter future that lets you navigate complex environments and come out a winner. Little goes under your radar as you discover excellent options.

MAY

26 Friday ~ Venus sextile Uranus 7:36

Today's sextile promotes a vibrant and active social life. With Venus charming and Uranus adding a dash of spontaneity to your weekend plans, it assures a fun and lively time shared with friends. An invitation to mingle brings a vibrant atmosphere that is ripe with potential. Being open to change and expanding your life into new areas creates a slipstream of potential that propels you to ever-increasing possibilities that nurture abundance and joy.

27 Saturday ~ Shavuot (Ends at sunset), First Quarter Moon in Virgo 15:22

Limiting beliefs block progress but soul-searching and releasing sensitive areas help heal the past. It broadens your perception of what is possible in your life when you push back the barriers. It brings a sense of liberation that cracks the code to a more abundant landscape in your life. It brings developments that nurture well-being and happiness. Life moves forward with ease as you head towards an engaging time shared with friends.

28 Sunday

Something important appears in your life soon. It marks a bold debut that offers unique experiences with friends and companions. Your inspiration burns brightly and lets you head straight for gold and turn the corner on a winning chapter. It aligns you with a shift forward that encourages personal growth and self-development. A trail of discovery sparks expansion and gives you something you can build. It lines you up with unique possibilities.

June

Sun	Mon	Tue	Wed	Thu	Fri	Sat
				1	2	3
4	5	6	7	8	9	10
11	12	13	14	15	16	17
18	19	20	21	22	23	24
25	26	27	28	29	30	

New Moon

Strawberry Moon

May/June

29 Monday ~ Memorial Day, Mercury at Greatest Elongation 24.9W

New options ahead hold a refreshing change. It brings a buzz of activity around your social life, allowing you to catch up with friends. Finding the right balance in your life increases harmony, helping you fully appreciate the possibilities ahead. Life sparkles with inspiration which marks a new beginning in your life. The pace picks up soon enough, bringing lively interactions and mingling opportunities.

30 Tuesday

Exciting news ahead brings a refreshing aspect to your social life. Opportunities to mingle help you advance life to greener pastures. It has a flow-on effect of nurturing well-being and improving the harmony in your world. Sharing with your circle of friends brings insight into new ideas which support your life. It takes you towards a sunny destination that grows your life outwardly.

31 Wednesday

Advancement comes calling, enabling you to receive positive feedback. You have been working hard to prove your mettle, and your dedication draws a pleasing result. Your willingness to pay attention to the details and strongly emphasize achieving a top result puts you in the correct alignment for growth as you head to rising prospects. It brings a more secure and stable environment that improves your bottom line.

1 Thursday

You enter a productive time that offers robust results for your working life. It reveals a lead worth investigating. Expanding horizons brings a new approach that elevates potential in your career. Life rooms with lighter energy as you chart a course towards a new growth pathway. Being methodical, laying the groundwork enables you to climb the ladder toward a successful outcome in your working life.

JUNE

2 Friday ~ Venus trine Neptune 22:42

Creativity and imagination are peaking under the blissful Venus, Neptune trine. Harmony, equilibrium, and well-being soar under this positive influence. Self-expression is rising, cultivating a unique path that captures the essence of artistic inclinations. Venus showers positivity over your social life, improving personal bonds. Information ahead initiates change as it brings a busy time that gets you in touch with your broader circle of friends.

3 Saturday

Following your intuition has you feeling lighter and more connected with developing your social life. This event pulls social engagement; it leads to developments and potential occurring around your personal life. It is a catalyst for growth and expansion. A sense of excitement hangs in the air; it brings a moment of bonding with another. It lets you remove blocks and shake free of any limitations that delay progress. It gets harmony flowing into your world.

4 Sunday ~ Strawberry Full Moon in Sagittarius 3:42, Mercury conjunct Uranus 19:50

Mercury and Uranus form a positive aspect that heightens mental abilities. Increasing mental stimulation promotes fresh ideas in your life today. Technology, messages, and communication all play a part in sparking inspiration and fostering possibilities for future development. Curiosity leads to an uplifting time discussing future projects and endeavors with a kindred spirit.

JUNE

5 Monday ~ Venus ingress Leo 13:42, Venus opposed Pluto 16:04

Your perseverance and dedication offer progress in your career path. It helps you push back the barriers and advance life forward as a new area opens up. Developing your skills brings a busy time of learning and growth. It helps you dive into uncharted territory and come out a winner. Stability increases, and this enables you to plan your course forward. It lets you blaze towards advancement as your skills shine brightly.

6 Tuesday

There is a lot of potential ready to flow into your world during this time. Opportunities ahead encourage you to grow and expand life outwardly. It helps you find balance in an uncertain situation by focusing on goodness and leaving the rest behind. Manifesting your happiness is on the agenda as you progress towards greener pastures. A time of discovery draws new options into your life.

7 Wednesday

You benefit from strategic planning as you prepare to plot a course around hurdles. It sets in motion improvement that offers advancement. It brings potential into your home life and lets you nurture your hobbies and develop an area of interest. A group venture ahead offers a favorable chapter of growth. A side hustle tempts you to learn a new approach as you crunch the numbers and come up with a winner.

8 Thursday

Welcome news arrives for you soon, bringing insight into an area that holds promise. You soon illuminate options that offer significant growth. It propels you forward towards developing your skills and using your talents. Enlightening discussions bring helpful advice. It draws movement and discovery that provides a transition towards an area of excitement. It teams you up with others who match your interests.

JUNE

9 Friday

Good luck arrives with a flurry of excitement. The rough edges that have caused friction in your mind soon fade. It brings a time of working to develop an area that ignites your inspiration. It brings a busy time which helps you move towards a meaningful goal for your life. A positive breakthrough comes calling, which enables you to map out a plan for future growth.

10 Saturday ~ Last Quarter Moon in Pisces 19:31

There is a lot of potential around the periphery of your life. You benefit from events on the horizon as it reveals a welcoming social aspect. Lively discussions and thoughtful ideas bring opportunities to mingle with friends. It leads to a happy time that nurtures grounded and secure foundations. Improving personal ties lets you spend more time with valued companions. It sparks insightful conversations that attract rising prospects around your love life.

11 Sunday ~ Mercury ingress Gemini 10:24, Mercury trine Pluto 10:27, Pluto ingress Capricorn 13:12, Venus square Jupiter 15:39

Today's Venus square Jupiter planetary alignment offers good things for your social life. It is the perfect time to engage with friends; lively discussions nurture creativity. It is a prime time for letting your hair down and having fun in a relaxing environment that draws stability into your world. It ushers in an impressive social aspect that cultivates sharing with insightful companions.

June

12 Monday

Expanding horizons ahead draws new options into your life. Fortune shines brightly over your situation as you reveal information that inspires growth. It offers an impressive pathway forward that helps you create a robust platform to grow your life. It provides a significant journey towards a meaningful area. Being receptive to change lets goodness into your life. Your pioneering attitude helps you blaze forward towards a successful outcome.

13 Tuesday

Information arrives that inspires change. It brings movement and discovery into view, which expands horizons most delightfully. Life moves faster; some unexpected twists and turns ahead see you navigating the path using wisdom learned. It brings new options flowing into your life that offer a chance to elevate your talents to the next level. A pathway opens, and this sees you reaching for a dream project.

14 Wednesday ~ Flag Day

An exciting aspect flows into your world and lightens the atmosphere. You connect with those out of touch, which paves the way toward a more lively environment. Entertaining and connecting with your tribe is a theme that resonates in abundance. It gets the ball rolling on an enriching phase of expansion that sees a personal goal taking shape. Remember, when you lay your bets via your intuition, things soon fall into place, drawing a pleasing result.

15 Thursday

You discover that things come together serendipitously. It brings clear skies overhead that nurture your spirit by expanding your social life. It creates the change that offers room to move in alignment with a long-held vision. You seal the deal by being open and nurturing the potential possible. Stability and security are the focal points that drive this situation forward. Growing your social life brings balanced foundations and can expand outwardly.

JUNE

16 Friday

Information arrives that gives you free rein to expand creatively. Past issues that left you feeling constrained and drained your energy soon dissolve under the luminescent possibility of new options. When an offer crosses your path, it connects you to others who share similar values and ideas. It brings a breakthrough moment that draws harmony. If you feel stuck in a holding pattern, new possibilities light the path forward.

17 Saturday ~ Saturn turns Retrograde in Pisces 16:52

Saturn is a planet that rules boundaries, structure, and discipline. This retrograde draws balance and righteousness into your situation. Making reasonable choices and decisions connects with karma to achieve a fair and beneficial outcome. Honesty, integrity, and impartial judgment are essential in making the right choices for your life. Facing the truth of a situation shines a light on the uneven scales. You see that everything works out for a reason.

18 Sunday ~ New Moon in Cancer 4:38, Father's Day (US)

You enter clearer skies and can embrace circulating with your wider social environment. Mingling in the community connects you to a refreshing level of abundance. Exchanging thoughts with kindred spirits expands your social life and rejuvenates your soul. News arrives that helps you release the heaviness and transform your vision towards a lighter chapter. A lovely time ahead hits a high note in your social life.

June

19 Monday ~ Sun square Neptune 3:53, Jupiter sextile Saturn 15:53

Today, the Neptune square Sun aspect can water down your ambitions, leaving you feeling foggy and indecisive. If your vision feels clouded, going back over your plans can help make sure they continue to align with your vision for future growth. Recommitting to developing your career goals can help shift some of the clouds that hang over your working life today. If the boss gives you a hard time, blame it on Neptune for bringing Monday woes into your working life.

20 Tuesday

You soon move in a direction that triggers a phase of growth. You are currently in a planning chapter that helps bring fresh ideas to the surface. As you dig more in-depth into your future goals, it brings a breakthrough that becomes a turning point for your life. Acting on a hunch helps you follow your instincts and head towards a brighter chapter. You soon break fresh ground, creating a space for new possibilities to blossom in your life.

21 Wednesday ~ Midsummer/Litha Solstice 14:58, Mercury sextile Mars 15:23

The Mercury sextile Mars aspect today fosters joint projects and cooperation. Getting involved with a group endeavor stimulates your mind and brings new possibilities. Brainstorming sessions offer a trailblazing path towards innovative solutions and rising prospects. Joining forces and strategizing with like-minded people cultivate an excellent success rate. It helps you cover the bases by blending other people's talents into the mix of potential at your disposal.

22 Thursday

Dabbling in evolving your abilities is therapeutic and nurtures well-being and happiness. It helps you unearth unique pathways of advancement which take your skills to the next level. It connects you with a broader social environment that offers kinship and companionship with like-minded trailblazers. The work you are doing to improve your circumstances draws a pleasing result for your life. It cracks the code to a caring and sharing environment with friends.

JUNE

23 Friday

You will soon receive what you need to thrive. Options ahead light an exciting path forward for your life. It draws a journey that offers connection, social engagement, and insightful discussions. Sharing with your broader circle of friends replenishes depleted emotional tanks. It helps you craft a journey that provides meaningful moments shared with friends.

24 Saturday

A new option arrives soon and tempts you towards expansion. It offers a journey of wisdom and grace as destiny comes calling. It sees you working with your talents and developing your skills in new areas. There is no need to rush this process as the journey is as important as the destination. A positive influence heightens your ability to manifest pleasing outcomes. It brings a time of inspired potential that leaves you feeling optimistic about the path ahead.

25 Sunday

Notable changes ahead highlight a path towards expanding your social life. A bond blossoms that draws peace and harmony into your life. Emotional awareness guides a fresh start that releases heaviness and removes outworn layers that limit progress. It creates space to focus on a situation that inspires your mind. It teams you up with a friend who brings a saving grace into your foundations, the giver of renewal and joy.

JUNE

26 Monday ~ First Quarter Moon in Libra 7:50, Mars square Uranus 9:22

New information brings signs and serendipity that offer a chance to merge your dreams with your aspirations. It brings a phase of gifts, luck, and good fortune. Setting intentions will help in ways currently unseen. It provides a goalpost that allows your creativity to take flight. It draws decisions that place you in the correct alignment to make the most excellent options that flow into your world. It brings a breakthrough, a eureka moment you can cherish.

27 Tuesday ~ Mercury ingress Cancer 12:22

Information arrives that has you heading towards a winning streak. It lets you stay on top of the game and explore new possibilities. It draws a busy and active time that connects you with others who share similar interests. The changes ahead keep you on your feet as a burst of new energy makes a dashing appearance in your social life. It brings an extensive chapter on developing goals and exploring innovative pathways that shape the course ahead in your favor.

28 Wednesday

News is imminent, which lightens your life. It brings upcoming invitations from your broader circle of friends. It highlights a self-expressive journey that raises confidence and sees you spending more time with companions who support your world. Creating a stable foundation to develop the sharing of aims and goals helps you connect with a rising aspect that offers abundance in your life.

29 Thursday ~ Sun trine Saturn 1:42

Today's Sun trine Saturn offers constructive dialogues and thoughtful ideas that enhance your creativity and stimulate new pathways of possibility in your life. A positive influence nurtures unique approaches that capitalize on the potential possible in your surroundings. Thoughtful discussions promote well-being and put a spotlight on harmony. Soul-stirring conversations usher in thoughtful discussions that re-energize life.

July

Sun	Mon	Tue	Wed	Thu	Fri	Sat
						1
2	3	4	5	6	7	8
9	10	11	12	13	14	15
16	17	18	19	20	21	22
23	24	25	26	27	28	29
30	31					

New Moon

Buck Moon

June/July

30 Friday ~ Neptune turns Retrograde in Pisces, 19:28

Neptune retrograde strips away delusions, allusions, and fanciful thinking. Under the glare of more informed thought processes, you build tangible growth pathways to take your talents to the next level. This phase enables you to sink your teeth into developing goals that offer fruitful results. Moving away from areas that have clouded your thinking and brought doubt to your judgment does provide you with clear stepping stones that take you towards success.

1 Saturday ~ Canada Day, Sun conjunct Mercury 5:05, Mercury sextile Jupiter 7:10, Sun sextile Jupiter 10:26

Open-mindedness, curiosity, and a quest for adventure are prominent aspects as a Mercury sextile Jupiter alignment fosters creativity and self-expression. This transit favors organization, planning, and the development of longer-term goals. Reviewing plans and streamlining your vision enables you to cut to the chase and find a practical path to progress your goals. New information emerges to catch your interest and spur you to advance your life.

2 Sunday ~ Venus square Uranus 14:32

An increased need for freedom and liberation can destabilize as Venus faces Uranus in a square alignment. Being mindful of balancing interpersonal bonds while being self-expressive and creative can ease tensions. At the same time, you can let your hair down and enjoy a freedom-driven chapter of fun and excitement.

JULY

3 Monday ~ Super Moon, Buck Full Moon in Capricorn 11:40

A therapeutic vibe enters your life as your thoughts turn back to the past. Understanding your journey helps you make sense of the challenges overcome. Indeed, everything happens for a reason; shining a light on challenging aspects nurtures healing and acceptance. Releasing sensitive areas offers a clean slate that promotes wellness. Being open to developing your life in a new direction draws significant improvement.

4 Tuesday ~ Independence Day

A refreshing change opens and heightens potential in your social life. It brings an optimistic phase that lets you make headway on planning for future growth. It ignites a bond that gets you involved in lively discussions. It releases the heaviness and helps you embrace nurturing a situation that offers lighter energy. It stirs up the heartwarming time that enriches your world. It brings excitement to the forefront of your life.

5 Wednesday

You kick off a cycle of good fortune soon that enables you to progress your dreams. You can break the restrictions that block forward momentum by being open to change and adapting to the circumstances you find yourself. New potential arrives, bringing the key to future growth. It shines a light on the vital energy that fosters more remarkable growth and prosperity in your life.

6 Thursday

You unlock the key to an essential chapter of growth. It enables you to overcome hurdles and break down obstacles that prevent progress. Take time to focus on areas within reach as it offers heightened security. It places you in a solid position to grow your dreams. You soon become busy with new assignments that provide pathways for growth and learning.

July

7 Friday

Life holds a refreshing change. It does help you clear areas that are ready for deletion and head towards a clean sweep of potential in life. Nurturing your abilities helps you grow a meaningful path forward, and this time investment lets you tap into the right track for progressing your skills to the next level. You see gratifying results that tick all the right boxes.

8 Saturday

Today shines a light on new possibilities as the path ahead clears. It marks a time of incoming information and communication that highlights new options that inspire growth. You are well-equipped to navigate a complex environment and reach the promised land. Improvement is looming overhead, bringing a sunny aspect into your world. You soon discover a climate ripe with blessings.

9 Sunday ~ Mercury trine Neptune 23:56

Mercury in trine with Neptune focuses on your dreams and goals; it adds mental clarity that helps you stay focused as you work towards realizing your vision. Something you hope to reach in your life can reach fruition with the correct planning, adjustments, and focus. Creating space to nurture your priorities lets you reap the rewards of a dedicated approach that offers an increasing success rate.

July

10 Monday ~ Last Quarter Moon in Aries 1:48, Mars ingress Virgo 11:34, Mercury opposed Pluto 20:47

A cutting-edge environment offers room to grow your career path. It takes advantage of innovative technology and brings new possibilities to your door. It lets you make a move that helps you power ahead. Your working environment expands as you launch into a chapter of big plans. You fuel inspiration with motivation. It brings advancement to your working life.

11 Tuesday ~ Mercury ingress Leo 4:09

An enterprising area brings a chance to rebrand your image. It grows your talents and harnesses creative thinking to set your sights higher. You raise the bar and learn an area that increases your knowledge and heightens your abilities. It gives you a chance to build a site that brings new possibilities into your environment. As you move forward towards advancing to the next level, you reshape goals and revolutionize the potential possible in your world.

12 Wednesday

You gain a glimpse of glittering possibilities and soon thrive in a busy and active environment. An area that has been on the backburner for a while gets the shift forward. It helps you sort out and organize the aspects of your life that have become disruptive. Streamlining and juggling demands draws the essence of efficiency to progress your life forward effectively. A powerful influence flows into your world, setting the stage for an enterprising chapter of growth.

13 Thursday

Life opens to a new flavor that lets you reach for more. An opportunity comes knocking; it creates space to chase a dream. As you take those first tentative steps to improve your situation, information arrives; it lets you hit your stride and progress forward. You gather the assistance of someone effective in evaluating ideas and offering advice. It brings a time of brainstorming sessions that see innovative solutions rising.

JULY

14 Friday ~ Sun sextile Uranus 23:02

In sextile with the Sun, Uranus captures the essence of surprises, new information, and discoveries. Something new and exciting is ready to manifest in your life. Being open to new people and possibilities charts a course towards rising prospects. Moving out of your comfort zone lets you create a journey that offers room to be a game-changer. Implementing proven strategies leads to a shift that provides a pleasing result.

15 Saturday

Exciting news arrives that gives you a chance to step up and share with friends. Manifesting happiness is on the agenda as a lighter approach draws sunny skies overhead. You share outings with valued companions as you blaze a trail towards a happy and supportive journey. Thoughtful communication offers a wellspring of abundance in your world. It cracks open a journey of kinship and companionship that bodes well for your future goals.

16 Sunday

A more stable landscape that helps you channel your energy productively into a meaningful journey forward. It draws an exciting landscape as new options arrive that support growth in your social life. Lighter energy triggers cascading possibilities to tempt you along towards nurturing your life. It brings a networking aspect that offers companionship with friends.

July

17 Monday ~ Mercury square Jupiter 12:48, New Moon in Cancer 18:32

The New Moon represents a creative seed of consciousness that promotes a fresh beginning in your life. It will bring a time of change and vision as you explore the infinite possibilities and potential around your life. You will feel increasing inspiration, curiosity, encourage that enables you to expand your horizons and explore new pathways. An unfamiliar element and zest for life will drive you forward beyond imagined limits as you head towards growth.

18 Tuesday ~ Islamic New Year

News arrives, which offers a chance to follow your passion. It takes your focus off the beaten track when you discover an enticing side journey that gives room to grow your abilities in a new direction. You enter a phase of learning and guidance that shapes the path ahead. It ushers in new energy that has you thinking about the possibilities. It inspires a stage of working towards a fixed goal, and expanding leads to a memorable phase that creates positive change.

19 Wednesday

There may be a sense of uncertainty holding you back. A time of self-discovery and contemplation brings the answers needed to move forward toward change. It initiates a stable growth phase that opens the floodgates to a happy chapter. Harnessing the magic in your life lets you use the power of your creativity to come up with viable options worth developing. A lead ahead brings movement and discovery.

20 Thursday ~ Sun trine Neptune 13:06, Mars opposed Saturn 20:39

The Sun trine Neptune alignment raises the vibration around your life. It focuses on improving the circumstances in your life and helping others who face difficult circumstances. Creativity is a valuable resource that lets you craft plans that offer tangible impacts that enhance your world. Life blossoms under your attention and care as you unearth new leads to develop. Change and evolution are part of the continual cycle that deepens your talents and grows your world.

JULY

21 Friday

News arrives that brings a boost. It offers a new project that focuses on working with your talents. Dabbling in a creative interest helps make the most of your capabilities as your talents shine when keeping busy. It offers a purposeful and inspiring path that cultivates your skills and advances life towards greener pastures. A positive influence brings a boost which sparks new options. It opens a journey that holds blessings and offers to revolutionize the potential possible.

22 Saturday ~ Sun opposed Pluto 3:52

The Sun shines a light on a hidden aspect Pluto keeps out of sight in your day-to-day life. This opposition Pluto creates a doorway through which pockets of the inner self, spirit, and primal energy can reach the surface of your awareness. It shines a light on subconscious desires and instincts. Life has an edgier aspect that can feel unsettling today. It does get you in touch with hidden depths that spark an internal dialogue as you reveal a personal element of your personality.

23 Sunday ~ Venus turns Retrograde in Leo 1:33, Sun ingress Leo 1:47

Venus turns retrograde, which slows the progress down around your love life. Romantic development slows down or stagnates during this phase. Focus on the building blocks as the journey is as important as the final destination. You ground yourself in the basics, and getting back to building a stable growth phase becomes a priority. As foundations improve, you nurture more balance in your love life.

July

24 Monday

News arrives that inspires change. Exploring pathways toward growth help, you unearth innovative options that allow you to develop creative solutions. It's all about thinking outside the box and growing the potential in your world. Life is ready to bloom, and this brings a boost to your inspiration. It heightens energy and lets you embark on a bold chapter of pushing back barriers and developing a goal of interest.

25 Tuesday ~ First Quarter Moon in Libra 22:06

Something new arrives that breathes fresh air into your life. It begins a golden phase of potential. You can gear up for a chapter of growth as you touch down on new options that advance your talents. It liberates tension and shifts your focus towards a productive and rewarding phase. Your skills blossom under a bright sky. It brings change and prosperity to your door.

26 Wednesday

You soon get wind of new information that unlocks essential news. It lets you move towards growth, and you may decide to reframe your goals when you reveal this aspect. It kicks off an exciting phase that sees life becoming lighter and more abundant. In this enriching landscape, you create space to grow your talents and nurture well-being by dabbling in an area that captures your interest.

27 Thursday ~ Mercury conjunct Venus 15:15

The Mercury conjunct Venus aspect today bodes well for your personal life. Communication flows, as does feelings, emotions, and sentiments. The time is right to share loving thoughts and receive positive feedback from someone who holds meaning in your life. Life takes on a rosy glow as you move forward toward new possibilities. It is a pivotal time to create change and open a new life cycle. Fresh beginnings leave you feeling inspired.

July

28 Friday ~ Delta Aquarids Meteor Shower. July 12th – August 23rd, Mercury ingress Virgo 21:29

There is a beautiful symmetry in the path ahead as it nurtures well-being and harmony in your world. Focusing on the building blocks of your life forms the basis of grounded energy. A new cycle is coming; it helps you shape the path by moving in alignment with your vision for future growth. A positive influence expands life and links you with kindred spirits in a social environment.

29 Saturday

There is an opportunity ahead that makes the most of your creativity. It brings an expressive chapter of dabbling in an interest that puts the shine on your talents. You secure foundations that draw stability and balance into your life. It brings a calming influence that releases external stressors, and it also brings opportunities to socialize with friends. It gets the ball rolling on an exciting chapter.

30 Sunday

A social aspect brings harmony overhead. It does offer an influx of possibilities that rules expanding your social life. Improvement on home territory becomes the main focus; it draws inviting potential that strikes a chord as it hits a positive note for your life. Additionally, exploring avenues of growth and creativity sparks tangible results. It gives feedback you can appreciate and develop as you plot a course towards new goals and endeavors.

August

Sun	Mon	Tue	Wed	Thu	Fri	Sat
		1	2	3	4	5
6	7	8	9	10	11	12
13	14	15	16	17	18	19
20	21	22	23	24	25	26
27	28	29	30	31		

New Moon

Sturgeon Moon

July/August

31 Monday

A goal you get involved with developing lets you establish your abilities in a new area. It draws an enriching landscape that sees you growing your talents as you head towards a busy chapter. Nurturing your skills feeds creativity and heightens the potential possible in your world. It opens a gateway forward that helps you map out new plans. It brings a time to pursue opportunities as choices act to trigger a journey that takes you closer to a lofty goal.

**1 Tuesday ~ Lammas/Lughnasadh, Super Moon,
Sturgeon Full Moon in Aquarius 18:32, Mars trine Jupiter 20:44**

An opportunity ahead rules greater happiness in your social life. It brings a time of cutting away from outworn areas. If you have been dealing with a toxic environment, going within and gaining clarity helps you see the truth of the situation. Seeing through the illusions around your situation helps cut through the confusion and dispel doubt.

2 Wednesday ~ Mercury opposed Saturn 2:16

As Mercury opposes Saturn, it brings heavy vibes into your life. The air of tension leaves a palpable sense of negativity around conversations and communication today. A serious-minded person may seek to have a strongly worded conversation with you. Setting boundaries and creating space to nurture the foundations in your life helps restore balance if talks become pessimistic today. Pushing business decisions off for another day is advisable.

3 Thursday

Changes ahead let you settle into a new groove. It brings surprises, twists, and turns related to your social life. A welcome surprise falls in your lap, and the effect is stable and nurturing. It helps you make effective changes that reflect your future goals and aspirations. It fuels motivation to engage proactively with your social circle. It helps form plans that connect you with kindred spirits, creating fresh possibilities.

August

4 Friday

Mapping out your vision underscores openness, which draws new possibilities to light. Striking while the iron is hot brings a bold moment that lets you create tangible progress. It brings communication that breathes fresh life into your social life. It puts a focus on freedom, abundance, and manifestation. It offers a luminescent journey that aligns with your dreams. It provides room to expand your situation and opens the path forward for new goals to emerge.

5 Saturday

Exciting new options flow in to inspire growth. It lifts troubles; the path ahead shifts and lightens. It brings the gift of expansion, activity, and inspiration. It all helps banish negativity and release outworn areas that limit progress. Being proactive advances your vision as you begin building rock-solid foundations. It brings a new start that lets you gain momentum on improving your circumstances.

6 Sunday

Getting involved in a grassroots project sees a project take off on the home front. Life enriches as you connect with joy. It's time to put your intentions into action and ground your energy in developing a project that inspires your mind. Getting anchored in working with your creativity draws wellness and abundance into your home life. It's a powerful tool for manifesting positive outcomes.

AUGUST

7 Monday ~ Sun square Jupiter 12:03

Today's Sun square Jupiter aspect raises confidence and brings good fortune swirling around your life. It does boost your ego, which could lead to you overstepping the mark. Knowing your capabilities and working within the systems you have in place for your life will help keep things in check during this energetic time.

8 Tuesday ~ Last Quarter Moon in Taurus 10:48

The more you expand and grow the potential that seeks to enter your life, the faster your talents blossom. Doing research brings new possibilities to light that offer a chance to develop your skills. News arrives that sparks a path of growth, learning, and wisdom. It kicks off a journey that provides the right environment for your abilities. Putting the shine on your talents draws a rewarding chapter that places you at a considerable advantage.

9 Wednesday ~ Venus square Uranus 11:09

A surprise element adds a sense of uncertainty to your personal/social life due to the Venus square Uranus aspect today. You may feel a restless component of your life calling your wild heart. Staying true to the energy that seeks expression in your life offers a spontaneous feature that brings a shift of priorities. Contemplating the options in your world offers a heartening glimpse of future possibilities.

10 Thursday ~ Mercury at Greatest Elongation 27.4 E, Mercury trine Jupiter 12:45

Mercury trine Jupiter today brings a boost into your life. Jupiter is the planet of good luck and fortuitous happenings, which improves the potential possible around your circumstances. You reveal curious information that opens the gate to a fresh start in your life. It focuses on the essence of adventure as you brainstorm ideas around future goals. It brings the chance to expand your circle of friends, and this companionship replenishes your emotional tank.

AUGUST

11 Friday

Things are on the move for your social life. Information emerges that brings an invitation to connect with social outings. You unpack a great time and bring new opportunities to light. Sharing with friends lightens the load and delivers a wellspring of possibility into your life. It helps you reawaken to the rich landscape of potential outside your immediate home environment. Life brings a group activity that nourishes friendships as you get busy expanding your life.

12 Saturday ~ Perseids Meteor Shower July 17th - Aug 24th

Fortune shines upon your life as you transition to a positive chapter that brings sunny skies overhead. Changes surrounding your social life ensure you are busy. New opportunities to mingle emerge, which helps you develop forward momentum. It opens the door to a social environment that enlivens and nurtures your spirit. It lets you spend more time with friends and share thoughts, leading to a collaboration ahead.

13 Sunday

Being open to new people and possibilities helps make a positive step forward in your life. You head towards a chapter that emphasizes growth. Constructive dialogues and lively conversations team you up with friends and companions. A sizeable gathering ahead brings a turning point as you bond with new people worth your time. It opens the gate to a busy and lively environment. Life is ripe with potential ready to bloom.

AUGUST

14 Monday

Your life is ready to move from strength to strength. A new project ahead offers excitement and sees the fires of your inspiration burn with creativity. It has you focusing on developing a dream goal. A bustling time of expansion draws well-being as life becomes lighter and more energetic. It offers impressive results for your life. It lets you establish grounded foundations that promote a balanced environment around your life.

15 Tuesday

Setting intentions and maintaining a positive outlook lets you take concrete action towards developing an inspiring area. It stirs up exciting potential and delivers an opportunity worth your attention. Setting the bar higher paves the way toward a rock-solid return. It ushers in a journey that focuses on nurturing skills and talents as you begin evaluating what is possible in your world. Advancing your abilities in a new area cracks the code to success.

16 Wednesday ~ Sun square Uranus 2:34, New Moon in Leo 09:37, Mars trine Uranus 13:53

Uranus steals the show today, and you can expect a spontaneous and expressive environment that offers a breath of fresh air in your life. Life ahead supports your efforts to improve circumstances. It keeps you on your toes as new possibilities draw an open road of potential. It lets you travel a journey that dazzles with exciting options, leading to a unique phase of growing dreams.

17 Thursday

Unexpected developments open the path wide to new possibilities in your career path. Nurturing this path offers room to progress your abilities to the next level. It draws security as it creates growth and prosperity. It propels your abilities forward and takes your vision to a new level of possibility. This news on the horizon is a morale booster; it sees life shaping up and heading towards an active and productive environment.

AUGUST

18 Friday

News arrives that expands your circle of friends. It offers a group environment and a chance to work with your creative abilities. A river of unique possibilities emerges in your broader social network, which becomes the gateway from which you grow your life. A positive influence reverberates around your life as it brings new options to your door. Your social schedule fills up with opportunities to mingle.

19 Saturday

There are changes in the air, revealing the social aspect that sees you sharing with friends and companions. Thoughtful discussions bring ideas and options which spark your interest. Getting involved with your broader circle of friends offers a secure foundation. It brings the room to inspire your creative levels. A purposeful push towards developing a goal brings forward momentum that charts a course towards a rising aspect in your life.

20 Sunday

Life brims with possibility and potential as you discover a new source of prosperity. It helps you attract the correct people who bring good energy into your life. You soon receive bright and cheerful news that makes you smile as you feel optimistic about expanding the borders of your life. It bolsters confidence and prepares you to engage with your social life's broader world of potential.

AUGUST

21 Monday

A change of pace arrives when information emerges that draws a boost. You discover an opportunity that has you daydreaming about the possibilities. It resolves issues by wiping the slate clean and kicking off a new growth cycle. A positive influence creates a smooth passage towards calmer waters that draw grounded and peaceful energy into your world. A new option is on offer, which marks the beginning of a journey worth growing.

22 Tuesday ~ Venus square Jupiter 12:13, Mars opposed Neptune 20:33

A Venus Jupiter square offers rising prospects for your love life. You will have trouble concentrating on the task as fun moments capture your attention. New energy is brewing in the background of your love life; it draws a vibrant atmosphere that offers social engagement. It brings the room to grow your life outwardly as changes ahead promote happiness and attract well-being and harmony.

23 Wednesday ~ Sun ingress Virgo 8:58, Mercury turns retrograde 19:59

Mercury turns retrograde and puts a damper on the potential possible in your social life. It can cause miscommunication and issues in your love life. Mercury in retrograde adds an element that turns communication haywire. It disrupts the positive flow of energy in your life. Delay signing contracts or committing to business deals during a retrograde phase. It is appropriate to plan and launch new endeavors after the retrograde cycle.

24 Thursday ~ First Quarter Moon in Sagittarius 9:57

You unlock the key to an essential time of growing your world in a new direction. A flash of insight and creativity directs your attention towards a refreshing option that takes you on a new journey forward. It lets you forge ahead as you discover a route that takes courage but offers advancement. Growing and evolving your talents enables you to tap into incredible results. A willingness to try new endeavors lets in the goodness.

August

25 Friday ~ Mars trine Pluto 12:22

Today's aspect offers rising prospects for your career. It brings a goal-orientated, disciplined, and centered focus on improving your working life. It is a great time that gets your goals and dreams on the front burner. A new project that lets you channel your energy productively. It heightens security and enables you to make notable tracks on improving the foundations in your life. A new cycle is coming that takes your aspirations further, and this hits the right note in your life.

26 Saturday

It's a great time to map out new goals and endeavors. The tides are currently turning in your favor. It brings a positive shift forward that lets you gather momentum towards developing your hobbies and interests. It enables you to dive into a chapter of fun and self-development. It has you exploring your options in a low-key setting that offers room to tinker with your ideas and develop a winning strategy.

27 Sunday ~ Sun opposed Saturn 8:28, Mars ingress Libra r 13:15

Life becomes plentiful, and new projects and endeavors spark your interest. It is a creative time that draws fun and friendship. A side project ahead taps into your artistic leanings and offers room to grow your world. It brings a memorable chapter of working on an area that energizes your spirit. It brings grace and harmony into your foundations, which offers improved security. You discover new possibilities to enhance your home life, and it gets a new chapter.

AUGUST

28 Monday

An idea you discover soon develops into a blossoming path forward in your life. It brings the chance to work with your abilities and design a journey that promotes your talents to a broader audience. Life settles into an enriching phase that helps you gain traction on advancing your skills. Grounding yourself in the basics lets you get involved with building a sound stage of rising prospects that progresses life forward.

29 Tuesday ~ Uranus turns Retrograde in Taurus 2:11

Uranus moving into a retrograde phase boosts idealism; it offers big sky pictures that help motivate change to improve the world around you. This planetary cycle will boost your confidence and foster leadership qualities. It deepens initiative and offers a fresh wind that spurs creativity and an uptick of potential. Prioritizing your goals adds a potent and robust aspect to the mix of manifestation in your life.

30 Wednesday

Opportunities to improve your circumstances abound. Being open to new possibilities captures the essence of manifestation. It lets you take advantage of the incoming potential that grows your abilities and takes your talents further. You are in a time of personal growth, guiding you to advance your skills into new areas. Positive news ahead re-energizes and lifts your spirits.

31 Thursday ~ Super Moon, Blue Full Moon in Pisces 1:36

Knowledge and wisdom into your future dreams help you plan a path in tune with your higher self. Your intuitive abilities assist you in becoming more aware of your desires. It enables you to find the areas in your life that are out of balance or lacking progression. Developing your life's journey helps you trust that your instincts will guide you correctly to the right situation for your life.

September

Sun	Mon	Tue	Wed	Thu	Fri	Sat
					1	2
3	4	5	6	7	8	9
10	11	12	13	14	15	16
17	18	19	20	21	22	23
24	25	26	27	28	29	30

New Moon

Corn/Harvest Moon

September

1 Friday

You have gifts that let you tap into new levels of potential. It charts an ambitious path towards using your abilities to achieve growth and improve your world's security. Intuition and creativity help forge the way forward. It brings new information into your life that transforms your world from the ground upward. Expanding your life draws luck, happiness, and joy. It lets you move forward with purposefulness.

2 Saturday

There is a shift occurring that brings fundamental changes to your social life. It takes you away from certain people in your broader social circle. As you drift away from areas that are no longer relevant, you begin a journey of developing a path that is in alignment with the person you are now. A vital component of this process is investigating new leads. It rules emotional awareness and trusting yourself to make the right decisions.

3 Sunday

Essential news is coming that points the way forward. This information enables you to blaze forward towards a self-expressive and happy journey. It brings fundamental changes that draw positive aspects to your social life. It connects you with people you value. This re-balances and rejuvenates your foundations. It has you moving away from outworn areas as it lets you spend time with a lively crew of people.

September

4 Monday ~ Labor Day, Venus turns direct in Leo 1:19,
Mercury trine Jupiter 10:29, Jupiter turns Retrograde in Taurus 14:14

Venus turns direct and brings an open road of potential into your love life. Delays that prevented progress no longer cause issues. It is a fantastic time to initiate new plans and improve your love life. Conversations and discussions ahead bring an active environment that fuels bonding—fun and companionship light up harmony in your world.

5 Tuesday

Going back to learning will bring new options into your life. It does help you chart a course towards rising stability that enables you to transform your life and head towards greener pastures. It will bring companionship and friendship into your social life as you discover kindred spirits who share similar goals. It lights a path towards a positive result, enabling you to gain traction on achieving an essential purpose.

6 Wednesday ~ Sun conjunct Mercury 11:08, Last Quarter Moon in Gemini 22:21

Independent thinking and innovative ideas can be attributed to the Sun, Mercury conjunct today. A new phase of life is coming that sees progression taking center stage in your life. It pairs you up with opportunities that head towards growth. It provides room to flex your creative muscle and dive into an expressive environment that develops unique goals. A time of learning the ropes of a new area draws expansion.

7 Thursday

There are opportunities ahead that let you improve the security possible in your life. A new chapter is coming that brings confidence and inspiration to the forefront of your life. It taps into your innate ability to discover options that grow your talents. Focusing your energy on improving your circumstances brings a path that delivers an abundant chapter. Expanding your life draws dividends.

SEPTEMBER

8 Friday ~ Sun trine Jupiter 11:12

The Sun forms a trine with Jupiter, which increases good luck and fortune in your life. A positive influence nurtures beneficial outcomes. A time of abundance and magic is looming. You head towards a chapter that glimmers with potential. Listening to your intuition holds you in the highest alignment to grow your life and achieve a fantastic outcome. You soon tap into a path of promise that continues a theme of expanding horizons occurring in your life.

9 Saturday

You are wise to stay open to new possibilities as this is the spice of life. A cornucopia of options flows into your world to inspire change. It stirs a vision that glimmers with refreshing options. An opportunity ahead brings a fresh wave of potential into your world that shines a light on companionship. It triggers a social aspect that brings bright and cheerful energy. It gets a boost that encourages lively and entertaining conversations.

10 Sunday

New information is ahead that lets you nurture an area that inspires your heart. It brings contentment, joy, and harmony flowing into your world. It does grow your life while expanding your horizons. It lights a path of inspiration that dissolves current limitations. It speaks of a refreshing change of pace ahead that draws new possibilities into your life. It brings a calming influence that helps release stress and resolve anxiety.

September

11 Monday

News arrives that opens the gate to a happy chapter. It draws a groundbreaking time connecting you with kindred spirits who share similar interests. An opportunity ahead offers a chance to study, learn, and grow your skills. It brings options to work with your creativity and develop your skills. It provides a sideline project to learn and grow. It does establish a grounded foundation from which to expand your world. It draws a trailblazing time of chasing leads.

12 Tuesday

News arrives soon, and it clears the clouds away, bringing lighter energy as sunny skies lift your spirits. Exciting potential brewing in the background of your life makes itself known and clears the slate clean. A fresh chapter ignites inspiration and allows you to reach for something more in your world. You enter an extended time of developing career goals and advancing your situation forward.

13 Wednesday

Game-changing information arrives that sets a positive trend, leading to unwrapping more options. It brings expansion and helps you make progress in your world. It ushers in change, and as life picks up speed, you sail through an active chapter. You investigate an area that offers a bumper crop of potential. It gives you room to expand your life as you unveil a positive aspect ahead.

14 Thursday

Change surrounds your personal life; being open to someone new kicks off a chapter of possibilities. Opportunities to mingle encourage a degree of expansion that shapes the path ahead. It offers a prosperous time for sharing thoughts and discussing items of interest with someone who inspires personal growth. These changes see life becoming more upbeat. It shines a light on information that helps you progress your vision for future growth.

September

15 Friday ~ Rosh Hashanah (begins at sunset), New Moon in Virgo 1:40, Mercury turns direct at 20:20

Mercury turns direct, and this improves communication and interpersonal bonds. It offers a renewed interest in your social life that helps harmonize frazzled tensions that occurred during the retrograde phase. It places your vision towards developing growth and happiness. It brings a transformation that provides to reshuffle the decks of potential in your life.

16 Saturday ~ Sun trine Uranus 1:23

The Sun trine Uranus aspect today adds a dash of spontaneity and excitement into your life. It is a favorable aspect that brings the freedom-driven chapter to light. Focusing on your social life draws a pleasing result as you connect with kindred spirits who offer excitement and passion. A sense of celebration lingers long after the event as you feel lighter and more connected with expanding your life. Rising confidence sees you getting involved in growing your social life.

17 Sunday ~ Rosh Hashanah (ends at sunset), Venus square Jupiter 6:12

The Venus square Jupiter aspect makes it the perfect day for unwinding and relaxing with your social circle. An easy-going vibe draws thoughtful conversations. Life settles into a more enriching phase that rewards you with growth. It refuels your emotional tanks and draws support as you deepen the potential possible in your life. Heightened security attracts grounded foundations that strengthen your life.

SEPTEMBER

18 Monday

New options help you craft a journey that utilizes your talents to stunning effect. It brings pathways of growth that raise the potential around your life. It promotes your skills and advances your abilities to the next level. It helps you extend your reach into a new area worth your time. A spotlight on working with your abilities brings a pleasing result. It enables you to restore stability in what has been an uncertain time.

19 Tuesday ~ Sun opposed Neptune 11:17

Your perception broadens as the Sun lights up Neptune's dreamy aspects. Engaging with creativity and imagination draws rising ideas and innovative concepts to consider. A potent mix of manifestation and inspiration brings the winds of change blowing into your life. It lets you build a grounded foundation from which to grow your dreams. It brings a happy chapter that rules expansion and harmony as you see an increase in your social life. Connecting with kindred spirits lights a busy path forward towards a remarkable destination.

20 Wednesday

Information lands in your lap that offers room to grow a dream. It places you in full strategy mode, which leads you straight to a journey of developing your vision. It brings a high-energy, quick-moving phase where you lay the foundations to progress an endeavor forward to the next level. Your efforts draw tangible results and put you in contact with other trailblazers. Brainstorming in a group environment gets you in sync with creativity.

21 Thursday ~ International Day of Peace, Sun trine Pluto 5:20

A burst of inspiration brings seeds of potential you can plant in fertile soil. It takes you on an enchanting journey that expands your horizons. This vibe is different from the work you have done previously. It brings exciting options for growth and prosperity. There is a learning curve to overcome. Leaning into challenges brings progress through discipline and hard work. An entrepreneurial theme weaves magic around your creativity.

SEPTEMBER

22 Friday ~ Sun ingress Libra 6:46, First Quarter Moon in Sagittarius 19:32, Mercury at Greatest Elongation 17.9W

There is a lot of potential surrounding your life, and this helps you break free of limitations that block forward potential. It brings a liberating time that offers freedom-driven, fun engagement with your friends. Getting involved with your social life sees enthusiasm rising. Lively conversations focus on supportive dialogues, which provide room to deepen friendships.

23 Saturday ~ Mabon/Fall Equinox 6:50

You open a clear path that soothes your restless spirit. You begin a soul journey that lays the groundwork for a secure foundation. As you continue to build and stabilize your environment, you discover projects that let you use your gifts and abilities to powerful effect. Your circumstances are improving, and this draws balance and emotional well-being.

24 Sunday ~ Yom Kippur (begins at sunset)

The atmosphere lightens, and you make room for new friends and companions. There is a focus on home and family; opportunities continue to flow into your life and teach you to grow and expand your skills. Offering your gifts to others lets you spread your wings. Life takes on a lighter tone; exchanges with friends bring an active and social environment. You build the memories that are moments to treasure.

September

25 Monday ~ Yom Kippur (ends at sunset), Mercury trine Jupiter 12:12

Today's Mercury trine Jupiter aspect brings optimism and good news. Research, learning, study, and socializing are favored. This trine is ideal for formulating new plans and engaging in future-orientated brainstorming sessions. It's also the perfect time to sort and organize; your office, workspace, closet, or even your whole life. It brings space for creativity to shine as you get busy and establish your talents in a unique area.

26 Tuesday

Being selective raises the bar. It helps distance from limiting areas that drain your enthusiasm. Be proactive about setting barriers as appropriate. Soul-searching draws clarity; it brings insight into the path ahead. A diverse track opens that brings unique characters into your life, laying the groundwork for expansion. It brings an influx of potential that offers time to nurture abilities. Change surrounds your life; a myriad of possibilities tempt you forward.

27 Wednesday

You head towards a chapter that re-invigorates your vision for future growth. It lifts flagging spirits and connects you with your social circle in a meaningful manner. It ushers in a theme of improving your circumstances that resonate beautifully with your future vision. A creative undertaking puts pioneering abilities to good use and elevates your skills in an area of interest. It creates a refreshing mix of potential, which expands your life outwardly.

28 Thursday

A new page opens in your book of life that initiates skills development. It broadens your talents as a prominent area tempts you forward. It helps you release your troubles and fire up inspiration as you extend your reach into a place that offers room for progression. It marks an important beginning that enables you to make a positive transition. It infuses your life with new dreams and possibilities.

October

Sun	Mon	Tue	Wed	Thu	Fri	Sat
1	2	3	4	5	6	7
8	9	10	11	12	13	14
15	16	17	18	19	20	21
22	23	24	25	26	27	28
29	30	31				

New Moon

Hunters Moon

September/October

29 Friday ~ Sukkot (begins at sunset), Super Moon, Corn Moon, Harvest Full Moon in Aries 9:58, Venus square Uranus 17:53

A restless vibe caused by a Venus Uranus square could undermine the security in your love life or the broader social environment if you are single. A freedom-loving vibration brings a need to be spontaneous and engage in unique adventures that change the day-to-day routine of your life. A strong emphasis on improving your circumstances promotes expansive horizons.

30 Saturday ~Mercury trine Uranus 16:56

Today's trine is perfect for using technology to keep life supported and flowing in your social life. Communication is your passageway to a more connected social life. Being innovative and thinking outside the box connects you with diverse pathways of growth and expansion. News arrives that brings a refreshing path. It offers a time for nurturing dreams as you evolve and grow on your journey forward.

1 Sunday

You set sail on a voyage that brings happiness and harmony into your life. Helpful news arrives, which illuminates a lively path forward for your social life. Additional opportunities to mingle make a busy and productive chapter. Sharing thoughtful information and nurturing discussions with friends draws insight into new areas worth your time and energy. A group project crops up which feels like a good fit for your life.

OCTOBER

2 Monday ~ Mercury opposed Neptune 3:34

The Mercury and Neptune opposition helps you communicate your ideas and thoughts today. However, You may find work challenging as rising creativity brings a desire to daydream. Taking time to pull back from extra demands and focusing on the building blocks of your life promotes harmony. It soon puts you in the direction that offers growth and progress. It brings time for developing goals and increasing wellness and enjoyment of pleasurable pastimes.

3 Tuesday ~ Mercury trine Pluto 19:20

You are entering a cycle of increasing possibility. You can make the best choices possible for your situation. Rising confidence helps you follow a journey that brings happiness into your world. It encourages you to move forward in alignment with growing your case as you get busy investigating leads that hold water for your life. Something ahead is ready to kickstart the journey of growth and progress in your life.

4 Wednesday

Exploring various avenues helps you reveal an exciting vista of pathways that grow your skills and nurture your talents. A time of discovery overhead draws options that build a path to extend your world outwardly. Your circumstances are continually evolving and changing. Moving away from areas that limit progress cracks the code to a brighter chapter in your life. News arrives to bring a boost into your life.

5 Thursday ~ Mercury ingress Libra 12:06

Mercury can bring an indecisive vibe that causes stagnant energy. Procrastination can be an issue that delays progress in the workplace. Focusing on removing distractions and streamlining your environment can help mitigate the effect of this transit. As you gain traction on developing goals, you create space for more stability to nurture wellness and harmony in your world. You pour your energy into a unique endeavor as you climb towards your goals.

October

6 Friday ~ Sukkot (ends at sunset), Last Quarter Moon in Cancer 13:48

Things are on the move in your life. You find an area to channel your restless energy into, which brings a time of unscripted adventures that lets you head towards unchartered territory. It fuels a social time that connects with your broader community environment. New possibilities emerge with a flourish, and this helps you progress towards a fascinating time filled with lighter and more energetic options.

7 Saturday ~ Draconids Meteor Shower. Oct 6-10

Your social life heats up with new possibilities and invitations to go out with your friends. Sharing with others solidifies the foundations in your life and helps build a happy path forward. Sunny skies emerge, bringing fun and lightness into your world. Cultivating interpersonal bonds launches life towards rising prospects. You soon generate an enterprising journey that inspires you to push back the barriers and expand your horizons.

8 Sunday

Life heats up with potential. You soon receive what you need to thrive as a social environment emerges to tempt you out with friends. You get a glimpse of a path that supports your dreams. It brings people into your life for a purpose, and this brings supportive energy that cultivates new friendships. It gets a chance to collaborate and nurture more excellent stability in your life.

October

9 Monday ~ Thanksgiving Day (Canada), Indigenous People's Day, Columbus Day, Mars square Pluto 1:04, Venus ingress Virgo 1:06

News arrives that illuminates a creative undertaking. You get busy with friends and hatch plans for future growth. It lets you nurture a journey that draws a stable foundation. It brings the chance to join a group project and progress your abilities into a new area. Riding a wave of hopeful energy, you feel lightness and momentum returning to your social life.

10 Tuesday ~ Venus opposed Saturn at 6:11; Pluto moves direct at 11:43

Information arrives that orientates you on a new journey. Investigating new leads brings a cycle of steady growth. It does tap into the essence of manifestation, and it helps you reach the stepping stones that let you achieve new levels of advancement in your career path. It has a powerful effect as it does provide you with a unique landscape of potential. It does see something on offer that brings good news.

11 Wednesday

A path of good fortune and luck flows into your life. News arrives that bestows blessings. It does link you towards an enterprising time that is active and creative. You tackle projects that inspire your mind, and this offers a remarkable chance to focus on areas that contribute to your sense of well-being. Improving stability and equilibrium brings a new level of possibility to light.

12 Thursday ~ Mars ingress Scorpio 3:59

Change is in the air, and fortune aligns to form a clear window to develop a new project. A phase driven by growth and inspiration draws prosperity and happiness. New goals and options tempt you forward. Making the most of this potential lets, you find a role that blends your abilities with your creativity. It does open your world to innovation and advancement.

October

13 Friday ~ Mars trine Saturn 12:28

The Mars trine Saturn aspect today boosts your working life. It enables you to gain traction on achieving a successful result. It puts the finishing touches on your working week as you meet deadlines with ease. This robust transit gives you the strength, ambition, and perseverance to take on the most complex tasks and complete them on time. Increased productivity and efficiency get the job done. Your self-discipline keeps you focused without being distracted or discouraged.

14 Saturday ~ New Moon in Libra 17:54, Annular Solar Eclipse 17:59

The New Moon encourages you to be proactive and open to new possibilities that seek to enter your life. Like the tributary seeks the ocean, your dreams will find a way into your life. Playing your part in this process does increase the odds of things happening sooner rather than later. Being open to new leads helps this process come together correctly.

15 Sunday

Change is swirling around your social life; being open to meeting new people draws companionship and support into your world. Enthusiasm and inspiration weave magic into your life as you resonate energy that attracts the right people. It helps you share meaningful dialogues, and this positive communication enables you to turn a corner and head towards growth. Opportunities to mingle are coming, which encourages a phase of expansion in your life.

October

16 Monday

You are on the right trajectory to grow your world. Information arrives that triggers an offer. It brings the news you have been waiting to hear. It opens the path towards developing a passion project and has a follow-on effect of jumpstarting advancing prospects in your life. The timing is sublime; good things are coming your way. It lets you start a chapter that offers room to grow a dream.

17 Tuesday

When news arrives, a refreshing change flows into your life that speaks of a new option that helps you push back barriers and create a bridge towards a brighter chapter. Keeping your eyes open helps you spot a diamond in the rough. It brings a time of chasing dreams and developing a plan that captures the essence of potential. Acting on instincts unearths positive news that flings open the doors to prosperity.

18 Wednesday

Some sort of unexpected news is likely to arrive out of the blue. This unanticipated information offers change. It does bring a time where anything is possible, and dreams emerge to have you thinking about the possibilities. Someone comes forward with helpful and encouraging advice. This person brings a gust of fresh air into your life. You feel supported and ready to face a more social aspect that lights the way forward.

19 Thursday

Words of wisdom and guidance light an enterprising path ahead. It brings information that shifts direction and brings excitement. It pushes back boundaries and lets you move out of your comfort zone and enjoy an active time of social engagement. Sharing ideas, thoughts, and discussions with your broader social circle helps you discover new information. You gently land in an enriching environment that offers support.

October

20 Friday ~ Sun conjunct Mercury 5:37

In conjunction with Mercury, the Sun is a favorable aspect that attracts communication. It is the best of all elements for receiving or sending communication. Interacting with others is vital today. It stimulates your need to share ideas and engage in thoughtful discussions that nurture well-being and harmony in your life.

21 Saturday ~ Orionids Meteor Shower Oct 2nd – Nov 7th, Mercury square Pluto 12:50, Sun square Pluto 14:09

Today's aspect causes a challenging environment as you find your judgment or authority tested. Being challenged and put to the test feels uncomfortable as you think you are making the right choices and decisions for your life. The Mercury square Pluto transit also attracts interactions with other people who feed the gossip mill and cultivate drama, leading to a toxic environment.

22 Sunday ~ First Quarter Moon in Aquarius 03:29, Venus trine Jupiter 4:32, Mercury ingress Scorpio 6:46, Mercury trine Saturn 16:12

The Venus trine Jupiter aspect offers golden threads around your social and love life. It is one of the most anticipated transits which harmonizes interpersonal bonds and offers rising prospects of good luck to your romantic life. It is of particular interest to those seeking love or lovers wanting a deeper romantic bond.

OCTOBER

23 Monday ~ Venus at Greatest Elongation 46.4W, Sun ingress Scorpio 16:17

Changes ahead bring expansion to the forefront of your life. It secures stable foundations as you get busy with your social life. Sharing with valued companions offers a supportive vibe that nurtures well-being. Freedom and expansion come calling, and you can let your curiosity guide you as you explore new growth pathways. It brings a busy time that launches your talents as you head towards advancing life forward.

24 Tuesday ~ Sun trine Saturn 7:13

Today's Sun, Saturn trine, gives you a commanding presence in the workplace. Confidence peaks in mid-afternoon, enabling you to effectively manage the day's tasks with relative ease as your energy keeps humming along productively. You conquer the workload and achieve a robust result with your consistent and disciplined efforts, which draw a pleasing effect and the added benefits of increased job satisfaction.

25 Wednesday

Information ahead enables you to progress your vision. It connects you with a more abundant chapter. Releasing blocks creates space to nurture your creativity. It does draw new possibilities into your life. It brings the essence of manifestation. It sees you settle gently into a new chapter that offers abundance. It does get a social environment that adds glamour to your life.

26 Thursday

You soon home in on new possibilities that offer growth for your life. It helps reshape goals as you head towards growth. A proactive approach draws a pleasing result. Unexpected developments ahead bring ample time for discovery. It offers room to advance your abilities and take your talents to a broader audience. Sharing your work with others emphasizes an expressive time that connects with identity and creativity.

October

27 Friday

You may feel a restless element in your life calling your wild heart. Staying true to the energy that seeks expression in your life offers a spontaneous feature that brings a shift of priorities. Contemplating the options in your world offers a heartening glimpse of future possibilities. Letting your emotions guide you forward enables you to nurture foundations as you head towards a purposeful chapter.

28 Saturday ~ Mars opposed Jupiter 16: 03, Hunters Full Moon in Taurus 20:23 Partial Lunar Eclipse 20:14

You can embrace one of the luckiest opposition aspects today when Mars opposes Jupiter and draws good fortune into your life. The winds of change carry news information into your surroundings. Today's transit increases your self-confidence and ability to handle your time and energy demands. It brings a competitive edge that fuels ambitions and the desire to achieve your goals.

29 Sunday ~ Mercury opposed Jupiter 3:44, Mercury conjunct Mars 14:21

Today, Mercury is the show's star and draws a favorable aspect that nurtures good fortune in your social life. It brings a chance to share with friends and loved ones. Relaxing and unwinding enable you to restore frazzled nerves and build robust foundations. It kicks off an engaging and happy time cultivating friendships and nurturing companionship. It brings invitations to circulate with friends, which hits a sweet note in your life.

November

Sun	Mon	Tue	Wed	Thu	Fri	Sat
			1	2	3	4
5	6	7	8	9	10	11
12	13	14	15	16	17	18
19	20	21	22	23	24	25
26	27	28	29	30		

New Moon

Beaver Moon

October/November

30 Monday

Transformation ahead brings the chance to wipe the slate clean. It offers you a real chance at achieving growth and happiness in your life. You enter a cycle of increasing possibility that leaves you feeling radiant about future options. Exploring new pathways jumpstarts a time of growth and prosperity. It lets you push back the barriers and head towards uncharted territory, where you discover a golden avenue.

31 Tuesday ~ Samhain/Halloween, All Hallows Eve Venus trine Uranus 12:51

Embrace a magical and vibrant Halloween under the influence of an engaging and dynamic Venus trine Uranus aspect that adds a dash of spontaneity and fun into your life. You are in a time of transition, and as the complications fade to the rear vision mirror, you remove the heaviness and usher in a clean slate of potential. News arrives, which inspires growth. It connects with sharing thoughts and ideas with those who value your contribution.

1 Wednesday ~ All Saints' Day

A wave of change initiates a positive trend in your life soon. It brings heightened confidence that lets you advocate for your vision. An area you begin to develop quickly takes flight and shows potential. It offers room to advance into the right path that provides a good return on time invested. A social aspect syncs you with kindred spirits who spark conversations that bring new information to light.

2 Thursday

You make notable tracks on improving your situation. Changes ahead shine a light on a viable option that lets you move forward. It does take your hopes and wishes further with a blend of manifestation and innovation. You attract something you have been searching to find. It does bring an opportunity that draws a happy chapter to light. A new cycle is coming that takes your aspirations further, which hits a sweet spot.

NOVEMBER

3 Friday ~ Sun opposed Jupiter 5:02. Venus opposed Neptune at 22:05

The Sun opposed Jupiter transit brings the increasing potential for wealth and good fortune. Rising prospects see things in your life fall in place as you turn a corner and head towards a lucky streak. The wheels are in motion to move away from outworn areas that limit progress. Fortune favors expansion, and life progresses towards an enriching time of developing unique goals. You refuel energy tanks and head off towards setting new goals that inspire your mind.

4 Saturday ~ Taurids Meteor Shower. Sept 7th - Dec 10th
Saturn turns direct in Pisces at 7:15. Mercury opposed Uranus 16:06

The Mercury opposed Uranus transit brings a chaotic and hectic pace. The busier pace may leave you feeling tense, anxious, and scattered. Uranus adds an unexpected dash, leaving you scrambling to deal with surprise news. Information emerges quickly, leaving you wondering what will happen next. Focusing on the basics improves balance.

5 Sunday ~ Last Quarter Moon in Leo 08:37

News arrives that expands your circle of friends. It offers a group environment and a chance to work with your creative abilities. A river of unique possibilities emerges in your broader social network, which becomes the gateway from which you grow your life. A positive influence reverberates around your life as it brings new options to your door. Your social schedule fills up with opportunities to mingle.

November

6 Monday ~ Venus trine Pluto 14:38

Today's Venus trine with Pluto adds intensity to your love life. This aspect turns up the heat in your personal life. Sexual attraction and passion rise as you get busy developing your personal life. Singles are likely to find new romance soon, while couples can embrace a more connected and sizzling love life. Circulating triggers a cascade of options that let you develop companionship in your life. It removes the heaviness and ushers in lighter and more vibrant energy.

7 Tuesday ~ Mercury trine Neptune 1:36

Creativity, imagination, and innovation blaze a wildfire of inspiration as Mercury and Neptune form a trine today. Increased sensitivity to this vibrational energy attracts a boost into your world that bolsters vitality. Life moves from strength to strength as you develop the path onward. News arrives that brings a bright flavor to your life. It flings open the door to a journey that grows your situation in a new direction.

8 Wednesday ~ Venus ingress Libra 9:27

The sun is shining overhead; it does bring a rich landscape into your world. It awakens the sense of adventure and lets you take in the new aspect that nurtures your creativity. It activates your talents, which is imperative as much growth and learning are ahead. A blank slate of potential lets you get involved in an inspiring area. You are wise to keep your energy open to new possibilities. There is a focus on expanding that blazes a path towards your vision.

9 Thursday ~ Mercury sextile Pluto 12:16

Today, the Mercury sextile Pluto transit adds extra layers and dimensions to your creative thinking. It brings an ideal time for research, planning, and mapping out unique areas for future development. Your penetrating inquiries delve deep and help you discover any potential pitfalls and issues. Your inquiring mind places you in a solid position to grow your dreams as you do due diligence and understand all aspects of your investigations.

NOVEMBER

10 Friday ~ Veterans Day (Observed), Mercury ingress Sagittarius 6:22, Mercury square Saturn 15:07

Today's Mercury square Saturn challenges critical thinking skills and intrepid enquiring. Tensions could flare up and lead to disruptions. Miscommunication is more likely when you are not on the same page as the person you talk to about your thoughts and ideas. There is some restructuring going on that they can feel challenging.

11 Saturday ~ Veterans Day, Remembrance Day (Canada), Mars opposed Uranus 21:11

The Mars opposed Uranus could catch you off guard today, leading to tension in personal bonds. An unexpected tension could flare up, causing an argument or dispute with a family member or loved one. If you find social interactions in your life under fire today, focusing on the basics and emphasizing clear communication can help bring stability back into your life.

12 Sunday

A shift forward brings a lovely boost to your world. It does highlight new options that encourage you to expand your horizons. You can create abundance by exploring all that life has to offer. A further possibility emerges that causes a great deal of excitement. It revolves around learning a new area, which creates a productive growth phase. You generate your leads and can go for gold.

November

13 Monday ~ New Moon in Scorpio 09:27, Sun opposed Uranus 17:20

The Sun opposed Uranus transit attracts a restless vibe that gives you the green light to try something new and different. It drives a liberating chapter that offers spontaneity as you get busy expressing your unique individual melody and personality. Being open to developing your social life expands your horizons in a more positive direction. Riding a wave of hopeful energy sees you taking action to boost your stamina.

14 Tuesday

Working with your talents creates a strong foundation that becomes the basis of security in your world. A busy and productive time ahead places the spotlight on developing your talents and growing your skills. It brings a fruitful direction to channel your energy as you advance to a new level of learning. The path ahead glitters with potential as you unpack a time of rising prospects that give you the green light to extend your reach.

15 Wednesday ~ Mercury sextile Venus 12:47

A loving vibe helps you get past hump day. Today's Mercury sextile Venus adds a positive influence that harmonizes and nurtures well-being in your world. Less stress and more enjoyment grow solid foundations. Personal relationships benefit from open communication leading to fulfillment. It offers friendships and social activities that draw well-being and happiness. You soon land in a refreshing environment that brings new possibilities to light.

16 Thursday

An opportunity arrives soon that brings a fresh way forward. You are wise to invest your energy judiciously. Focusing on the areas that bring the greatest happiness is a surefire way to take your abilities to the next level. A gateway forward helps you map out a plan for where you need to go. Nurturing your skills feeds your creativity and heightens the potential possible.

November

17 Friday ~ Leonids Meteor Shower November 6-30th, Mars trine Neptune 8:36, Sun trine Neptune 14:51

Under the influence of Neptune, creativity soars, epiphany's and lightbulb moments are the order of the day. It helps you gain traction on developing goals as you discover an opportunity previously hidden from sight. Investing in your talent brings a happy time that offers secure foundations. It lets you widen and grow your skills as you extend your reach to a new area.

18 Saturday ~ Sun conjunct Mars 5:41

Sun conjunct Mars brings abundant energy and initiative, and your drive to try new things increases. A desire for action can cause restlessness if not channeled and released. The more you push back the barriers, the easier it becomes to assert yourself and pursue your dreams. Laying the foundations for improvement holds the key to a new growth cycle. Expanding opportunities offer a trailblazing journey forward toward rising prospects.

19 Sunday

A new possibility emerges soon, capturing your interest. It is the right area for your life; unearthing this lead brings an industrious chapter that offers room to grow your world. It highlights a social aspect that brings co-conspirators and companions together in a group environment. Lively discussions blend trailblazing ideas and reveal a time of planning that is a precursor to growth.

November

20 Monday ~ First Quarter Moon in Aquarius 10:50, Sun sextile Pluto 21:26

Today's Sun sextile Pluto transit drives ambitions and sees you heading into the working week with an increased drive to succeed and conquer your goals. Feeling determined and purposeful enables you to nail your tasks quickly and finish work with energy still in the tank. Your willingness to explore leads brings a positive result. It opens the gateway toward growth in your working life. You soon get busy developing skills and learning the path ahead.

21 Tuesday

You soon enter a busy time that emphasizes improving circumstances. You build life one brick at a time, keeping foundations secure and balanced. The energy of manifestation swirls around your environment, helping you turn a corner and develop your life in a new direction. Working with your creative abilities nurtures well-being and has a profound effect on improving your life. You touch down in an environment that draws conversations with friends.

22 Wednesday ~ Mars sextile Pluto 1:17, Sun ingress Sagittarius 13:59

Today's transit increases energy in the workplace. No job is too small as you take on the lot and work towards your vision. It brings a valuable reward for growing your life outwardly. Amid a time of change, you discover a journey that captures the essence of luck. It cultivates new options that break up stagnant patterns as you develop your skills to the next level.

23 Thursday ~ Thanksgiving Day (USA), Sun square Saturn 9:46

Saturn is the ruler of honoring traditions and following rigid structures that form set boundaries. Today's square illuminates a happy time shared with loved ones, perfect with Saturn, who delights in honoring the past. Creating space for inner reflection can help you connect with insight and information. Weeding out distractions and nurturing some quiet time enables you to hear the wisdom within. Something tempting arrives to breathe fresh air into your surroundings.

November

24 Friday ~ Mars ingress Sagittarius 10:10

This transit emits a rebellious vibe that rejuvenates your energy and has you seeking expansion. You certainly can create an upgrade in your life by unearthing leads and connecting with others who provide advice and support. Changes ahead nurture your talents and advance your skills. It brings a focus on growing your life, and this bodes well for developing a new enterprise. Sharing your talents with a broader audience brings rising prospects.

25 Saturday ~ Mars square Saturn 16:57

Today's aspect can feel challenging as your mind is on Saturn's to-do list. You may find it difficult to relax and unwind when your thoughts turn to the irons you have burning in the fire. A bustling time of crafting your vision lets you get busy with expanding life outwardly. You gain traction on developing growth. An emphasis on advancement brings a pleasing result. It draws a goal-orientated chapter that helps you climb the ladder in your working life.

26 Sunday

Lovely changes ahead promote a change of pace as an invitation emerges to mingle. It brings an uptick of potential for your social life. Exciting news arrives that gives you a chance to step up and share with friends. Manifesting happiness is on the agenda as a lighter approach draws sunny skies overhead. You share outings with valued companions as you blaze a trail towards a happy and supportive journey.

November

27 Monday ~ Beaver Full Moon in Gemini 09:16, Mercury square Neptune 13:26

Today, the Mercury square Neptune aspect can distort or make mountains of molehills. It adds a dash of illusion into your business dealings that can have your head spinning with tall tales and trying to sort the truth from the exaggeration. If something appears out of line with your practical thinking, give it a miss. It's essential to do due diligence and avoid shady areas that only cloud your judgment.

28 Tuesday

Being open to meeting new people opens your life up to possibilities that offer growth and companionship. It does push back the barriers and heads towards the time of nurturing friendship in your life. It brings a lively and dynamic environment into your world, which grows a path that facilitates a sunny aspect in your life.

29 Wednesday

You enter a busy time ahead that sees your schedule filling up. Streamlining and refining help maintain efficiency during a lively chapter in your life. In this dynamic and active environment, you discover pathways that offer growth and abundance. Laying the groundwork of your life stably and thoughtfully opens your world to new possibilities. It brings an enriching time that provides a fresh start in your life.

30 Thursday

Focusing on the essentials takes you towards an exciting chapter. A goal you get involved with lets you establish your talents in a new area. It helps you progress your vision towards new possibilities. It kicks off an exciting chapter where life becomes greener and more abundant. In this lush and enriching landscape, you grow your talents and head towards a busy environment.

December

Sun	Mon	Tue	Wed	Thu	Fri	Sat
					1	2
3	4	5	6	7	8	9
10	11	12	13	14	15	16
17	18	19	20	21	22	23
24	25	26	27	28	29	30
31						

New Moon

Cold Moon

December

1 Friday ~ Mercury ingress Capricorn 14:29

The tides turn; you can prepare for a positive shift that brings new options into your world. It does draw an exciting opportunity to develop a path of wisdom and learning. Developments around your life offer progression; it does align you towards achieving a goal you have had in the background of your life for quite some time. It brings a new attitude and perspective as you see things are finally shifting forward.

2 Saturday ~ Mercury sextile Saturn 15:25

Today's Mercury sextile Saturn transit is favorable for organizing and streamlining your workload to create a stimulating and productive environment. Expressing authority and leadership skills create a purposeful and productive environment. Doing research and exploring new pathways brings high-level options into your life. Opportunities ahead offer a newfound project that becomes a source of inspiration.

3 Sunday ~ Venus square Pluto 13:29

Today's aspect could see a flare-up of jealousy or possessiveness. Your romantic partner may feel threatened by heightened social activities and invitations in the pre-run up to Christmas. Take time to support and boost confidence to help offset the Venus square Pluto aspect. Being aware of these fears' dynamics helps keep relationships healthy and balanced.

December

4 Monday ~ Mercury at Greatest Elongation 21.3 E, Venus ingress Scorpio 18:48

A lighter influence flows into your social life by drawing an engaging chapter shared with friends. It facilitates and promotes expansion in your world. Sharing interesting conversations and outings sees your life consistently becoming livelier and more social. Life picks up momentum as invitations crop up that inspire change. It does provide a rich environment for your personal life as you get busy developing romance in your world.

5 Tuesday ~ Last Quarter Moon in Virgo 05:50, Venus trine Saturn 22:51

Today's Venus trine Saturn transit is ideal for developing relationships. Self-expression, warmth, and affection flow freely under this favorable aspect. Being receptive to change rejuvenates and re-energizes your spirit. You discover a journey that promotes wellness and harmony. It offers a vibrant time to nurture the foundations and develop social bonds.

6 Wednesday ~ Neptune turns direct in Pisces, 12:38

With Neptune turning direct in Pisces, an extra emotional element adds flavor to your dreams, creativity, and vision. Wistful thinking, goals, and fantasies let you move beyond the material world and escape into fanciful thoughts about future possibilities. It shines a light on growing a creative enterprise. Working with your talents draws a nurturing influence that releases outworn areas and builds stable foundations that rebalance and rejuvenate your life.

7 Thursday ~ Hanukkah (begins at sunset)

A friend from the past is thinking about you and hopes to get in touch soon. This person feels you have a stable influence and an engaging personality. They bridge the gap to grow a journey that involves catch-ups and thoughtful conversations. It brings more communication and potential flowing into your social life. Invitations, news, and engagement carry you forward to greener pastures.

December

8 Friday ~ Mercury trine Jupiter 4:04

Mercury's trine Jupiter transit today ignites the possibility of heightened intuition and attracts a chance to chill with friends. Immersing yourself in a social environment balances your foundations. Communication and activities nourish your soul and connect with your tribe. Life brims with new possibilities to improve your world. You strike gold by getting involved with your social life. It smooths over the rough edges of your life and brings companionship.

9 Saturday

You touch down on a fascinating landscape that lets you spend time with friends and kindred spirits. It brings a uniquely uplifting time of sharing thoughtful dialogues. It enables you to develop a path that promotes happiness and harmony in your social life. Invitations to circulate let you meet new people. A busy environment ahead allows you to make the most of a lively and engaging chapter that promotes sunny skies overhead.

10 Sunday ~ Venus opposed Jupiter 3:34

This astrological transit adds an indulgent vibration and has you wanting to explore hedonism, romance, and magic. The pursuit of pleasure attracts social engagement, relaxation, and unwinding with a leisurely influence restoring well-being. Good news flows into your life. It helps you lay the groundwork to improve the security in your world. Focusing on your vision for future growth lets you make the essential changes that offer rising prospects in your life.

DECEMBER

11 Monday ~ Mercury sextile Venus 19:22

Communication flows freely into your social life, attracting invitations and mingling opportunities. The Mercury sextile Venus aspect nurtures stable foundations and happiness. It brings the green light to pour your energy into achieving a top result. Building sound foundations encourage balance and attract happiness. Opportunities to socialize with friends bring a happy chapter.

12 Tuesday ~ New Moon in Sagittarius 23:32

You discover an open road of exciting options that tempt you forward. It brings a burst of sunshine into your world. It offers new possibilities that help you power ahead using skills and abilities. Newfound motivation fuels inspiration and enables you to launch into a new chapter of significant gains for your life. It leads to a richly creative environment that sets up a stable foundation from which to grow your life outwardly.

13 Wednesday ~ Mercury turns Retrograde in Capricorn 7:08
Geminids Meteor Shower Dec 7-17th

Mercury turns retrograde, seeing some communication issues cropping up over the next few weeks. Plans and times quickly become mixed as messages scramble during this more chaotic planetary phase. The wheels are in motion to move away from outworn areas that limit progress. You are in a time of transition; you can remove the heaviness and usher in a clean slate of potential.

14 Thursday

The positive news is imminent, which helps lift the barriers that hold you from achieving your best. A unique path because your name and your willingness to try new things draw a pleasing result. Expanding horizons sees a new approach in your life draw dividends. Good fortune is due in your world; it soon flows into your life and helps you reach for a dream you've had for some time.

DECEMBER

15 Friday ~ Hanukkah (ends at sunset)

Your social life begins to pick up and become more active and dynamic. It sparks a ray of sunshine that helps you reinvent life from the ground up. It lets you take advantage of some of the options in your broader community. You explore the potential around your social life and plant the seeds for a journey that facilitates growth and happiness. A companion offers insightful conversations.

16 Saturday

A social aspect ahead rebalances your spirit and draws rejuvenation into your world. It brings a lighter influence that feels like a step in the right direction. It brings lively discussions, and this wellspring of support in your broader social environment draws healing energy which nurtures your spirit. A spotlight on promoting your life highlights a time of social engagement, stimulating conversations, and entertaining activities.

17 Sunday

You may feel nostalgic at this time, and focusing on your home life becomes a substantial emphasis as it promotes more outstanding balance and stability in your life. Planning future goals opens a doorway that lets you step along the path toward improving life. You touch down on a supportive environment that links with social engagement. Mingling and networking help crack the code to a brighter future.

December

18 Monday ~ Mercury trine Jupiter 14:33

Mercury trine Jupiter transit brings optimism, luck, and good news. Information arrives that bodes well for your social life. Indeed, it's easy to make new friends under this favorable influence that sparks social engagement and thoughtful discussions with friendly characters. Incoming communication increases potential in your social life. It shines a light that nurtures brilliant talks and mingling with valued companions.

19 Tuesday ~ First Quarter Moon in Pisces 18:39

News arrives that leads to expansion as you discover your curiosity is sparking to know more about this area. It adds a social element that adds fun and excitement to share with friends. It brings ample time to expand horizons that help you forge ahead towards an engaging time. Spending time nurturing your extended social life draws companionship, promoting well-being and happiness.

20 Wednesday

Today brings harmony and happiness into your life that nurtures companionship. Sharing news sparks a journey that stimulates growth in your life. Pushing back the borders of your life opens your world to a newly confident and joyful approach. It generates a time of lively discussions and opportunities to entertain with friends. Thoughtful communication offers a wellspring of abundance in your world.

21 Thursday ~ Ursids Meteor Shower Dec 17th – 25th, Venus opposed Uranus 7:04, Mercury sextile Saturn 12:35

Today's Venus opposed Uranus alignment brings growth to personal relationships. Increasing synergy and chemistry could spark a new romance or flirtation opportunity. A change of direction brings more incredible blessings into your life. It triggers a positive change that takes your vision further. A pathway opens for your life; this becomes a focus for you moving forward.

December

22 Friday ~ Sun ingress Capricorn 3:24, Yule/Winter Solstice 03:28, Sun conjunct Mercury 18:53

The Sun conjunct Mercury aspect favors communication. It brings the sharing of thoughtful dialogues and entertaining discussions. A time of transformation heats a lighter chapter that offers social engagement and community involvement. It launches a time of promoting stable foundations as you get busy with new projects and endeavors on the home front.

23 Saturday ~ Mercury ingress Sagittarius 6:19

News arrives that expands your circle of friends. It offers a group environment and a chance to work with your creative abilities. A river of unique possibilities emerges in your broader social network, which becomes the gateway from which you grow your life. A positive influence reverberates around your life as it brings new options to your door. Your social schedule fills up with opportunities to mingle.

24 Sunday ~ Sun sextile Saturn 17:28

Sun sextile Saturn transit lends patience to family gatherings, which can be a godsend if your family dynamics tend to be challenging. Moving away from drama and areas that have become stale aligns you with a journey that ushers in new possibilities. You open a gateway towards a happy phase of developing your social life and connecting with others who reflect your values. Sharing thoughtful discussions leaves you feeling settled.

DECEMBER

25 Monday ~ Christmas Day, Venus trine Neptune 17:15

Venus trine Neptune transit is the perfect backdrop to Christmas. It attracts creativity, well-being, and fulfillment. This transit favors singing, music, and delight in the day's celebration. It promotes confidence and enables you to step into a new chapter that initiates growth in your life. Dazzling potential tempts you out of your comfort zone, placing you in a stronger position to enhance your world.

26 Tuesday ~ Kwanzaa begins

Lovely changes ahead promote a change of pace as an invitation emerges to mingle. It brings an uptick of potential for your social life. Exciting news arrives that gives you a chance to step up and share with friends. Manifesting happiness is on the agenda as a lighter approach draws sunny skies overhead. You share outings with valued companions as you blaze a trail towards a happy and supportive journey.

27 Wednesday ~ Cold Full Moon, Moon before Yule in Cancer 0:34, Mercury square Neptune 7:36, Sun trine Jupiter 15:28

The Sun trine Jupiter aspect lights up good fortune across the board. New possibilities blossom as a favorable wind ignites your passion and imagination. It takes you on a comprehensive journey; it encompasses an extended time of increasing your life in new directions. It ultimately brings a better sense of purpose into your world. It lights a path towards an abundant landscape.

28 Thursday ~ Mercury conjunct Mars 0:26, Mars square Neptune 22:15

The Mars square Neptune aspect brings gossip and scandal to your ears. You hear surprising news that feels disconcerting. If it doesn't ring true to your ears, you should do your own investigating. This transit could draw misinformation leading to confusion. Tall tales and scandalous gossip attract shaky foundations in your social life. Focus on what you know about people and give the whispers a miss today.

December

29 Friday ~ Venus sextile Pluto 6:00, Venus ingress Sagittarius 20:21

The Venus sextile Pluto transit deepens romantic love and grows relationship potential. It brings an expressive time of nurturing a wellspring of abundance in your world. Life resonates as you kick off a time of lively discussions. Invitations to circulate draw vibrant talks and opportunities to bond. News and information ahead light the path forward. It highlights a time of freedom and adventure that strongly emphasizes promoting personal bonds.

30 Saturday

Looking deeper and beyond the surface helps you remember the unlimited possibilities within your spirit. Listening to your quiet voice for advice lets you know the right area to instinctively progress. Beginning a new trail can feel mysterious and daunting but leading with your instincts points you in the right direction. It cracks open a journey of kinship and companionship that bodes well for your future goals.

31 Sunday ~ New Year's Eve, Jupiter turns direct in Taurus at 2:41

In a promising sign, Jupiter turns direct on New Year's Eve. It foretells bright blessings, good fortune, and opportunities on the horizon. Unlimited possibilities spark inspiration and wonder in your life. Reawakening to the magic and potential of working with your creativity helps develop a plan for future growth. Working with your skills brings assignments that align you towards development.

Astrology & Horoscope Books.

https://mystic-cat.com/

Made in United States
North Haven, CT
19 March 2023